trotman

HILARY NICKELL

Internet

UNCOVERED

Internet Uncovered

This first edition published in 2009 by Trotman Publishing, a division of Crimson Publishing Ltd., Westminster House, Kew Road, Richmond, Surrey TW9 2ND

© Trotman Publishing 2009

Author Hilary Nickell

British Library Cataloguing in Publication Data
A catalogue record for this book is available from the British Library

ISBN 978 1 84455 175 0

Typeset by RefineCatch Ltd, Bungay, Suffolk

Printed and bound in Great Britain by
Athenaeum Press, Gateshead

trotman

Internet

UNCOVERED

Careers Uncovered guides aim to expose the truth about what it's really like to work in a particular field, containing unusual and thought-provoking facts about the profession you are interested in. Written in a lively and accessible style, *Careers Uncovered* guides explore the highs and lows of the career, along with the job opportunities and skills and qualities you will need to help you make your way forward.

Titles in this series include:
Accountancy Uncovered
Art and Design Uncovered
Charity and Voluntary Work Uncovered
E-Commerce Uncovered
The Internet Uncovered
Journalism Uncovered, 2nd edition
Law Uncovered, 2nd edition
Marketing and PR Uncovered
Media Uncovered, 2nd edition
Medicine Uncovered, 2nd edition
Music Industry Uncovered, 2nd edition
Nursing and Midwifery Uncovered
Performing Arts Uncovered, 2nd edition
Sport and Fitness Uncovered, 2nd edition
Teaching Uncovered
The Travel Industry Uncovered
Working For Yourself Uncovered

CONTENTS

About the Author

Hilary Nickell is a careers consultant, trainer and author with specialist knowledge of the use of the internet and interactive media. He project manages Career Companion Online, a regularly updated professional and student review service of web-based information at www.careercompanion.co.uk.

Previous publications include: *Career Change,* which he co-authored with Alison Dixon; three editions of *Surfing Your Career*; and for a number of years was editor of *Careers Resources on the Worldwide Web*. He also regularly researches web-based information on behalf of Connexions and the Nextstep organisations.

Prior to launching his own business – Surf In2 Careers – eight years ago, Hilary was senior information officer with VT Careers Management, formally Hampshire Careers Service. As a careers adviser he provided guidance to young people in Alton and Liphook as well as British nationals in seven European schools.

In a former life Hilary was a Royal Marine commando and residential social worker with Dr Barnardo's.

Acknowledgements

I would like to take this opportunity to thank a number of people who have helped me enormously with *Internet Uncovered*, including the following:

Chris Hutchinson	web developer, Whitelight Creative
Chris Wallace	Open University student
Graham Wood	Hazelwood Sound and Vision
John Nickell	undergraduate, University of Glasgow
Simon English	web designer, Whitelight Creative
Toby Grimshaw	Careersinfo Ltd

And of course none of this would have been possible without my wife Alison and our family John, Peter and Mark, who sacrificed and supported me so much through many a long day and early dawn. Also, my dear brother Rodney whose encouragement is a constant source of inspiration.

Hilary Nickell
August 2008

INTRODUCTION

Have you noticed that just about every new game or communications device must now also interact with the internet whether it's the latest Nintendo Wii, PlayStation, Xbox games console, BlackBerry, or Apple iPhone? Even our home PCs are fast developing into super media players with improved interactive programme choices such as the BBC iPlayer, which had over 42 million downloads in its first three months. The use of web cams has grown with the take-up of Microsoft Messenger and Skype in both home and office environments; the web cam itself has gone from optional extra to full integration, built into monitors. All these developments have been enabled by greater broadband speeds, heralding better graphics, more content and additional interactivity.

Clearly, the demand for more flexible access to an ever-increasing range of information is growing at a phenomenal pace as friends, family and interest groups join the latest trends in social networking. While younger people largely led the way with sites such as MySpace and Bebo, there is increasing evidence that Facebook, originally more popular with older students, is now also extensively used by adults. A further good example is Saga Zone, which had 30 000 early registrants who are now creating blogs, joining forums and sharing photo albums. This, together with the increased confidence in and success of internet shopping and the arrival of internet TV, demonstrates the successful coming of age of web-based information and services.

However, as well as increased personal and social interest in using the internet, there are also exciting and newly created internet careers. This highly innovative and creative sector is responsible for introducing many new types of jobs never imagined just a few years ago. Also, jobs once exclusively found in computing, information technology (IT) and telecom businesses are now represented right across the whole commercial and industrial landscape of the nation and global marketplace.

How about this timely quote from one of our case studies on page 32:

'The industry is evolving at an incredible rate. It's moved from being a fringe technology to the core of all mainstream business in only a few years.'

WHO SHOULD READ THIS BOOK?

This book has been written to meet the information needs of:

- school and college students

- graduates

- jobseekers

- career changers

- teachers, careers advisers and parents.

HOW IS THIS BOOK GOING TO HELP ME?

Throughout this book we will be providing you with fascinating facts, and a series of jargon busters to help with some of the strange IT initials and acronyms. We will also help you with the often confusing and overlapping range of job titles. However, a useful place to start this publication is to consider in more depth the new technologies that are likely to have an impact on our personal and professional lives as well as on the employment trends in this rapidly expanding sector. You will discover in Chapter 1 that, while few statistics are available about internet jobs specifically, the wider, related IT and telecom industries can provide a useful guide to current and likely future trends. The same chapter, also looks in greater detail at the range of organisations you might work with. The internet provides for secure, fast and efficient data transmittal. Collaborative work is made easy by the versatility of the internet; its arrival has created the opportunity for thousands of people to work from home or access work out-of-office. Its versatility in turn increases its importance and our dependence upon it. It's available from almost anywhere, 24 hours a day, 7 days a week!

The range and diversity of applications that the internet supports is rapidly developing, so Chapter 1 will also provide a helpful overview of some of the successful current technologies as well as looking at some new ones. These include the current expansion of Wi-Fi and WiMax, the latest interest in ultra mobile PCs, internet protocol television (IPTV) and voice over internet protocol (VoIP) and the likely fusion between on- and offline applications. Most of these will all have an impact on the future job market and the wider opportunities you might be considering. Chapter 1 will also investigate the effects of globalisation, increased enterprise and concern for the environment, and the significant changes the internet has brought to the traditional workplace.

Once you are clearer about the dynamic nature of this sector, Chapter 2 will identify the many different jobs which are either unique or common to four distinctive internet careers sectors. This will include technical and scientific roles – related to how the internet works – and design and audiovisual jobs – more concerned with appearance and how the internet looks. Content and information roles will also be covered, including jobs involving the preparation of materials and their presentation from a user perspective, followed by commercial and marketing roles which relate more to how the internet might sell products and services. Chapters 3 to 6 explore these key jobs in greater depth. Each chapter will include where possible average salaries, the good and bad aspects of a particular job as well as the personal skills and qualities suited to a given type of work. In this way, we hope you will really begin to uncover what it is like to work in a particular field or specialist role and the prospects offered for advancement and increased salary. We have also added a number of personal case studies so that you can get a real insight into different careers.

Home-working and self-employment opportunities have significantly increased with developments in information technology, but, as you will discover in Chapter 7, the impact of the internet is also creating new and exciting types of work. You will discover that jobs that were once only possible in a particular location are now as easily carried out in cyberspace – anywhere in the world!

Chapter 8 will examine the wide-ranging training and qualification routes for a career in the internet, including the new 14–19 Information Technology Diploma. It is here that you will begin to identify what is likely to be your preferred type of training. It may be that you like the idea of working with an organisation that already has established training structures or that you prefer to enter the workplace later after a mixture of academic and/or vocational skills development in further and higher education.

The final chapter will help you plan the next steps towards preparing for an internet-related career. It will also help your further research by providing details of appropriate websites for the material in each chapter and refer to other potentially helpful publications. Yes, a feast of enticing delights awaits your reading and surfing pleasure!

Good Luck!

FASCINATING FACT

In 1973, University College London and the Royal Radar Establishment in Norway become the first international connections to the ARPANET (Advanced Research Projects Agency Network) in the USA – the forerunner of the internet.

CHAPTER 1

Technological advances and employment trends

Without doubt few technologies have had greater impact on mankind over the past 10 years than the internet and its ability to network computers and all manner of applications across the globe in the time it will probably take you to get up from your chair! Furthermore, hardly a week goes by without some new internet-related innovation being announced on the news or streamed through your RSS (really simple syndication) feed. While it is therefore difficult to predict employment trends with any certainty and even more so to try and forecast new roles, it is still possible and important to anticipate likely changes. Also, it is reassuring to appreciate your own potential – should you enter this sector – to transfer or 'up-skill' your experience to meet the technological demands of the future. This is explored in greater detail in Chapters 3 to 5 when we look at the wide-ranging creative, technical and/or scientific skills needed to support diverse industries. Shortly, we will explore the employment sector further, but first let's have a closer look at how recent and new technological trends have already established themselves and are fuelling ever greater innovation.

SOCIAL NETWORKING

Facebook is probably the latest and best known social network phenomenon. Following its launch in 2004 as a student social networking utility, its usability ensured rapid expansion to form a diverse, adult user base, with users in various educational, geographical and work-related communities. The facility to set up events, blogs and forums is creating niche interest groups and some interesting challenges for Facebook and other successful social networks tempted by new 'interest targeting' revenue opportunities. For Facebook, classified ads already allow users to sell and purchase products and advertise events within their geographical location or social community; at the moment online businesses generally deal directly with customers, but it could be that certain goods and services find themselves marketed and distributed almost entirely via social networks in the future. The banner ads, currently provided to Facebook by Microsoft, could soon be supplanted by more-targeted advertising.

In the United Kingdom and Canada, Facebook has more members than any other social networking site, whereas in America, MySpace still dominates. MySpace tends to attract a younger membership, as it allows users to alter the appearance of their profile using HTML (hypertext mark-up language) code. MySpace also appeals to those with an interest in music. With a database of over eight million artists' pages, the site has been credited with the making of bands such as the Arctic Monkeys and the breakthrough of Lily Allen. MySpace has targeted its advertising for some time, reportedly receiving high revenues for doing so, although no official figures are released by the owners Fox News Corporation.

It may come as a surprise that, despite each site attracting well over 100 million users, MySpace only employs approximately 300 people directly and Facebook about 500 to set up and run their sites, develop new features, monitor advertising revenue, control usage abuse and generally operate their businesses. The challenge for such businesses, organically grown from small beginnings, is not to keep pace with market developments, but to set the pace within a market of users prepared to migrate from one free service to another. They need to offer ever more usages and increasing accessibility for their platforms, without losing the essence and essential purpose of their services which have made them so popular with users in the first place.

BLOGS

This increasingly popular open forum communication tool enables users to write an up-to-date chronological e-journal of their thoughts. Depending on the website, blogs can either be very personal or can perform a crucial function for an organisation or company. There are three basic varieties of blogs: those that post links to other sources; those that compile news and articles (like the BBC blog); and those that provide a forum for opinions and commentary. Importantly, all blogging formats offer the reader the opportunity to interact with the material. No longer is the reader passive, instead the view that content is enhanced by the expression of broad responses and divergent opinions abounds. Peer-to-peer review exercises are considered an effective way to ensure the accuracy of material. The blogging sector perhaps reaches its most personal where the user can be assured that only those known to them can access their opinions and commentary: this is the case when the blog is incorporated within a social networking site. Nonetheless, social interest and workplace networks are also forming at a phenomenal rate. Often these offer opportunities for jobseekers to gain informative insights into certain careers, insights that would never have been possible a few years ago unless industry contacts. If you are thinking of setting up a blog, a good place to start might be by looking at David Armano's '4 Cs to blogging – community, clarity, consistency and content'. See Futurelab http://blog.futurelab.net.

PODCASTING

Podcasting was once the delivery method of exclusively online audio content via an RSS feed. In one sense, it's like radio on demand, however, in reality, podcasting gives far more options in content and programming than radio as listeners can determine the time, place and programmes they want to receive, often by subscription. Listeners can then retain audio archives of podcasts such as 'Spanish lessons', 'Ask a biologist' and others, podcasts offering learning opportunities to be listened to at the subscriber's leisure. While blogs have turned many bloggers into journalists, podcasting has the potential to turn podcasters into radio personalities and video podcasters into television presenters! Podcasts must be downloaded from the internet, and as podcasting tools.com says, they are often accompanied by a blog offering opportunities for interactivity.

ONLINE PUBLISHING AND BUSINESS-TO-BUSINESS PUBLISHING

The internet has radically influenced the publishing world to the extent that traditional publishers will struggle if they don't adapt to new technologies or changing online-savvy customer needs. Demands are made of newspapers and news sites: our appetite for news is undiminished; we need updates as events unfold. We then want to bookmark or share articles with friends and family, have some means of articulating our views or commenting on other people's, and save personal preferences into sites so our news of interest is served to us. Not that long ago there was quite a strong negative reaction to reading text online, however, with considerable improvements to web design, presentation of content and the arrival of the LCD (liquid crystal display) experience, the perception that reading large amounts of text on screen is uncomfortable, impractical or unsatisfactory is changing or has changed. Publishers have to follow the advertising revenue, which is moving online at a pace.

Business-to-business (B2B) publishers are successfully finding niche markets and targeting content to the needs of their professional audiences, while at the same time providing prime customers to advertisers. Printed trade magazines are expensive to produce and distribute so there is a growing trend for delivering content directly into the specific applications.

For the individual, the era of exciting self-publishing opportunities has also taken root with sites like www.lulu.com offering no set-up fees to produce paperbacks, hardcover books, photo books, calendars and cookbooks to individual taste.

E-COMMERCE AND E-MARKETING

E-commerce has rapidly established itself within business as well as family life as individuals' experience and confidence in trading online increases with new security measures. Use of sites such as eBay is commonplace, but also booking holidays and banking online are becoming increasingly popular for the 24/7 convenience of managing one's leisure time or finances from home, or indeed from any PC. The financial sector is set to innovate further as there is evidence that by locking customers into an electronic service, they are not only less likely to move their accounts, they will also consolidate deposits and other financial activity at the provider of the online service. E-marketing (see also Chapter 5) expenditure in the UK broke the £2 billion barrier in 2006 thanks to a 41.2 per cent surge in growth accompanying increased usage, along with marketers' realisation of the potential to match promoted goods and services to site content. The internet has heralded a transformation of the way in which consumers and producers interact; a new era of marketing communication and consumer behaviour has been brought about by the user-generated content that high-speed broadband take-up has created.

FASCINATING FACT

Just coming off the drawing board is new internet software that lets you deposit paper cheques by taking their picture with your mobile phone and transmitting the images to your bank.

E-LEARNING

There is no universally accepted definition of e-learning, but the following is used by the Chartered Institute of Personnel and Development (CIPD): 'Learning that is delivered, enabled or mediated using electronic technology for the explicit purpose of training in organisations.' What is without question is the phenomenal growth in learning materials now being delivered through the internet rather than by CD-ROM. While the Open University (OU) and distance learning providers have long been pioneers of online learning, a greater range of professional course-based materials are also beginning to impact on the workplace. Further improvements in technology and interactivity are likely to increase demand still further.

MULTI-PLATFORM DEVICES

At one time software producers aligned themselves with particular methods of delivery, but increasingly it is recognised that it's important to develop multi-platform applications that can run on any device – mobile phones, personal organisers (personal digitals assistants or PDAs), PCs, internet televisions – and perhaps also be connected to the houses of the future with built-in monitors to manipulate the environment. Currently, you have to check your mobile or PC to see if there are any messages. In the future, your mail will find you through more versatile devices acting in compatibility with each other, siphoning off messages according to your set preferences. For example, you might be waiting for an important personal message which might then appear on your television, kitchen monitor or electronic newspaper. To the end user, the technology involved might soon go unnoticed, 'cross product protocol' agreements ensuring seamless delivery.

Microsoft, while late to release purely web-based applications, leapt to the forefront of multi-platform technology with the launch of the new Live Mesh service in 2008. Mesh is designed to connect a multiplicity of devices and applications, creating an online network so that files, folders, music and photos can be transferred with ease between, for example, your PC and mobile phone. Mesh is also compatible with Apple Macs (Microsoft's main competitor). The opportunity to interact remotely between home, work and mobile software applications anywhere in the world is a good example of how power is being granted to the user. The increased accessibility of information will have a dramatic effect on the shape of the job market, with more and more individuals opting to work from home. In addition, opportunities for businesses to coalesce will undoubtedly increase dramatically, and this co-operation will bring its own new challenges.

As you continue reading about current and likely future technological developments, it is important to note that new and as yet unknown roles are likely to develop in the future.

VOICE OVER INTERNET PROTOCOL

Sometimes referred to as 'internet telephony' or 'voice over broadband', this technology allows users to make free or relatively cheap phone calls over the internet. Excitingly, it is still at an early stage of development. Some websites already offer direct VoIP links on their sites, whereby one can 'click-to-call' a customer service representative if in need of assistance. Providing useful statistics for the website of when users choose to call a representative, this can then direct improvements to a webpage's design, clarifying areas to reduce call volumes. Bandwidth efficiency and low costs mean that VoIP is likely to own a large slice of the corporate telephone market before long. Already network operator 3 has launched a Skype phone that enables users to make calls using the online service through their mobile phone – the Skype service already being popular for making calls from PCs. Video calling is likely to feature in future devices. Visit www.voipreview.org for more information.

FASCINATING FACT

A UK Scientist Tim Berners-Lee is recognised as inventing the World Wide Web whilst working with CERN (European Organization for Nuclear Research), a European project located in Geneva.

WINDOWS MEDIA VIDEO FORMAT

Windows media video (WMV) format was designed by Microsoft to handle all forms of video content and is an excellent way to get file sizes down to reasonable levels while still retaining viewing quality. Careersbox has made a significant impact in the UK and is the foremost free supplier of WMV formatted careers films. These can be easily downloaded directly to classroom PCs or the home. At time of writing, seven IT-related careers films could be viewed at www.careersbox.co.uk.

There are a number of excellent providers of IT careers videos. E-skills is a specialist government body for this sector, supplying detailed descriptions of various jobs in the IT industry. Filming for the web is one of the fastest growing developments, with an increasing number of websites beginning to include short films to introduce their product or service. Unfortunately, it is too early to identify career routes, but we have included an important Case Study at the end of Chapter 5 to indicate the value of developing appropriate experience where possible.

WI-FI

Wi-Fi, through the use of unlicensed-spread-spectrum radio technology, has made the internet more accessible, useful and available than ever before. Wi-Fi is useful in allowing local area networks (LANs) to be deployed between client devices without numerous cables, wires, switches, adapters, plugs and connectors; reducing the costs and complexity of network deployment and expansion in offices and homes. Open access wireless networks in cafes, hotels and motorway services gives access to a high-speed internet on the move. A global standard, Wi-Fi succeeds in ensuring compatibility and co-existence of devices worldwide.

Wi-Fi, simplistically a radio transmitter that is plugged into a broadband internet connection, has a reach that extends to 30 metres indoors and 100 metres outside. This is a necessary limitation though, as with increased mobility, speed of connection falls. WiMax (see below) may be more mobile and global system for mobile communications (GSM) more mobile still, but the speed decreases with each.

Wi-Fi therefore, currently facing no significant competition, is becoming more popular and well renowned, and is now cementing its dominance through delivering broadband internet to computer games consoles, allowing gamers to interact and compete with each other worldwide. Furthermore, 500 million Wi-Fi-enabled handsets are predicted to be sold per year by 2012 (source: ABI Research, 2007). This growth is driven by the flexibility and convenience of Wi-Fi combined with the increased popularity of VoIP. Voice over Wi-Fi here we come!

WIMAX

This wireless technology can provide high speed broadband over long distances. With greater range than Wi-Fi, there is also an argument that it is a more reliable carrier for VoIP, as quality of service (QoS) is said to be more constant; WiMax users once connected are assigned a slot, whereas Wi-Fi simply connects users contentiously, with users competing for access. WiMax is already big in the US and some areas of the developing world, such as in Nigeria, and is set to grow in Europe too with a European Commission Order made on 21 May 2008, demanding that member states make frequencies available for WiMax.

Milton Keynes has just launched what it claims is the first WiMax powered wireless internet city in the UK. The WiMax Forum anticipates that WiMax will grow by 13 per cent in the next five years; this will be more than 133 million users globally by 2012 (WiMax Forum www.wimaxforum.org).

INTERNET PROTOCOL TELEVISION

Internet protocol television (IPTV) has been hampered in the past because broadband speeds were not fast enough to deliver a reliable service. According to an IPTV World Forum report (www.iptv-forum.com) over half of all homes in Britain now have broadband. Crucially, medium speeds are increasing with ADSL2+ (asymmetric digital subscriber line) becoming operational on progressively more carriers throughout 2008. Alongside established services from BT Vision and Virgin Media, other operators are cashing in on providing lines, with mobile phone operators O2 and Orange getting in on the act. We are also seeing the merger of PC and television technologies with the BBC introducing its highly popular iPlayer, allowing individuals to catch up on its output over the web. This was quickly followed by Channel 4's 4oD and ITV's Catch Up services.

Jargon Buster

ADSL   asymmetric digital subscriber line – high-speed technology suitable for downloading digital video and audio content through telephone lines using special modems.

B2B   originally describing business-to-business transactions conducted electronically, usually online, the term has gained in popularity and no longer refers purely to e-business.

digital native   a person born after 1984 who has always been surrounded by the culture of online technology. Often compared to digital immigrants who had to learn their way around the internet.

DSL   digital subscriber line – telecommunications line that provides a fast, permanent connection to the internet.

hotspots   locations for wireless internet (Wi-Fi).

HTML   hypertext mark-up language – as opposed to a programming language, HTML uses tags to structure text for webpages into headings, paragraphs, lists and links.

Windows   a series of software operating systems produced by Microsoft. First a graphical user interface (GUI) add-on to MS-DOS released in 1985, Microsoft Windows has evolved into an operating system that dominates the world's personal computer market.

ISP   internet service provider.

mashup   when a website draws on data from multiple sources (including an external one) but presents the data by one single integrated tool. Mashups create the opportunity for new and distinct web services, such as those sites offering price comparison of multiple retailers which cannot be provided without referencing and incorporating multiple web sources.

portal   website designed to be a user's main point of entry to the internet. A portal provides diverse and user-directed content, as well as navigational assistance to tempt users to make it their homepage.

RSS   really simple syndication uses a standardised format (XML – extensible mark-up language) to publish regularly updated text or media content such as podcasts, blog entries and news headlines, enabling subscription of users via email or media application.

tags   code that describes a command or instruction so that a web browser can interpret and display it. It is evolving as a way of organising and sharing web-based information such as social tagging.

Web 2   or Second Generation Web refers not to a change in the technical specifications of the internet, merely to the change in software developers' approach to and users' demands of the internet. Mashups, wikis, widgets, blogs and podcasts are all good examples of Web 2 applications.

web browser   a software program that can be used to view, download, upload, surf or otherwise interact with text, images, videos and music on the internet. Internet Explorer, Netscape, Mozilla Firefox, Safari, Konqueror, Opera, Flock, Epiphany and AOL Explorer are examples.

widget   application that usually sits at the top of a website offering users additional interactive features and found commonly in social network sites. Examples include photo slide shows, videos and music play lists.

wiki   website that allows users to easily add, remove or edit content.

Many of the above jargon busters have been reproduced by permission of © 1994–2008 NetLingo ™ The Internet Dictionary *at http://www.netlingo.com.*

MOBILE PHONES

We have already seen that mobility and technology go together and, as hand-held devices become increasingly sophisticated, manufacturers are competing for greater market share. Nokia is certainly up with the best, taking 40 per cent of all mobile phone sales in the last quarter of 2007. Its new N-Gage devices will offer customers a greater gaming experience with over 30 choices, blurring further the distinction between business and pleasure on what were once purely communication devices. This is also an area that Apple is moving into with the iPhone, launched in 2007, which has numerous features including voicemail, ring tones, SMS (short message service), photos, music, video, Wi-Fi, email, maps, widgets, multi-touch, and the revolutionary wireless accelerometer, which senses the orientation of the phone and changes the screen accordingly. Also, the latest 3G iPhone is looking to compete with the already highly successful BlackBerry with its multipurpose Microsoft business applications and emailing facility. It's possible that science fiction will take another leap into reality as mobile phones before long may have the facility to alert shoppers to special retail sales offers. What next?!

AIR, GEARS AND SILVERLIGHT

One of the largest drawbacks of any internet-based application is that they can only be used when there is a connection and, while we are seeing some improvements in speed total, ever-present connectivity is still a long way off. However, necessity (being the mother of invention) has encouraged the blurring of the online and offline worlds. In the past year a number of technologies such as Air (Adobe), Gears (Google) and Silverlight (Microsoft) are beginning to impact on the way people access what normally would be exclusively web-based information. This is partially due to the increasing digitalisation of written and image-based materials so making it possible for these new technologies to take rich web content and make some of it, or even most of it, available offline.

So, when the user next goes on the internet, possibly just to check emails, any updated information will automatically transfer from the host organisation to the offline materials. In practical terms, one of the best examples is an eBay desktop application which uses Air and lets the user design and set up auctions offline. When the user next goes online, their listing is automatically uploaded to the website. Silverlight turns this round by offering users the ability to build desktop applications to then run in a web browser. Gears allows normally web-based functions to be taken offline. We are likely to see more examples of such applications using one of these three tools in the future.

Reality Check!

We hope by reading this chapter you have begun to appreciate that behind the latest and very exciting technological developments are also a wide range of job roles in areas such as:

● **research and development**

● **design**

● **manufacture**

● **marketing sales.**

If you are into the internet, social networking and love using your PC and gadgets generally, it may be that a career in the internet could be of interest to you. *Or* is it more for social interests, generally a good time-waster and fun thing to do? Would you be happy working to strict time scales, within a fixed budget, constantly changing technology and client expectations? If the answer to the second question is yes, then read on as we look at the employment trends already being felt in this sector.

EMPLOYMENT TRENDS

Having explored briefly the impact of recent and new internet-related activity and technologies it will be helpful now to begin looking at their likely impact on some of the employment sectors that might appeal to you. We will take a brief look at five principle sectors: business administration; computing and IT; creative and media; finance and selling; and engineering and sciences. Don't be surprised to see that the internet is influencing just about every profession.

BUSINESS AND ADMINISTRATION

It is estimated that around 27.4 per cent of Britain's workforce is employed in business or administrative jobs across every single industry and that this represents 4.4 million people. The jobs are in all types of occupations, such as accountancy, tax, business or management consultancies, market research or the legal sector. They can also be in businesses, to do with selling or renting properties, advertising, recruitment or personnel. Employment in every one of these sub-sectors has risen over the last year. Clearly information technology forms the backbone to the success of such diverse businesses, with increasing reliance upon secure intranet (web-based) internal support as well as new e-commerce and e-marketing services. Estate agency is an interesting example as the opportunity to view properties online whether in the UK or overseas has now become the norm. So, if you are at the early stages of exploring careers ideas, perhaps it is a good time to consider whether it's the use of the internet as a tool in business you are likely to enjoy most, or whether you want to develop a specialist technical or scientific skill in IT.

COMPUTING, IT AND TELECOMS

It is important to remember that a job in IT may not necessarily involve the internet, as we can glean from an e-skills UK report in 2006 which mentioned that over 20 million people in the UK use IT in their daily work. This is likely to have increased since then as we have become increasingly reliant upon technology to meet most of our information and communication needs. Around 1.4 million people work in this sector with many in IT departments of businesses in a variety of industries – including hospitals, local government, manufacturing etc. In addition, an estimated 804 000 people work in over 115 000 registered businesses whose sole function is IT related – including telecoms, consultancy, database activities, equipment repair and maintenance, and call centres. Clearly, again, not all these people are working exclusively with the internet: program developers, for example, could be working on bespoke in-house systems. What you can assume, however, is that within the many and diverse job sectors mentioned above there will be internet-related roles for web designers, web developers, content administrators and managers, as well as, in many businesses, online marketing and sales opportunities. We will be exploring qualifications further in Chapter 8, but the most recent Annual Business Inquiry survey noted that 63 per cent of the jobs in the industry are at management or professional level – much higher than the average for the economy as a whole – and 94 per cent of businesses employ fewer than 11 members of staff. So, despite the large organisations mentioned earlier, there is a strong likelihood that you might be working with a very small specialist business if pursuing an IT career and perhaps move between organisations regularly if you wish to widen your skills portfolio (source: www.itjobswatch.co.uk/jobs/uk web%20development.do).

FASCINATING FACT

**A total of 508 000 new jobs are likely to be required between 2004–2014 in the IT industry and these do not include IT jobs in all the other industries that employ IT staff.
Source: Institute of Employment Research.**

CREATIVE AND MEDIA

While there are few tangible statistics available on internet-related careers specifically, we can glean from some trends that web-based applications are likely to play a significant if not absolutely crucial role in the success of a wide range of creative industries. As mentioned in the introduction, the exciting developments in the BBC's offering of listen and view again for local and national programming is leading the way on harnessing web-based technologies. The creative skills of web designers are at the forefront of most industries as businesses have to offer a web presence to their market if they are to compete effectively. Workhound (www.workhound.co.uk) is one of the UK's largest job search engines, listing thousands of jobs from all the major job boards, agencies and employers. At the time of writing over, 700 web design vacancies were posted, with the majority of jobs in London and the South East – a useful reminder, as with many jobs, that you need to consider where you are prepared to work and how far you'll travel for the right job with good prospects for the future.

FINANCE AND SELLING

This differs from the business and administration heading above in that we can see that a great deal of internet-based activity specifically involves buying and selling new and used products. Highly successful examples include sites like Amazon and Play. com with some individuals actually running small enterprises on the back of regular eBay purchasing and sales. This shopping revolution has also successfully impacted on other industries, such as transport, with courier firms collecting and delivering increasing amounts of goods to the home. This, together with the larger retailers investing heavily in developing their online shopping experiences, suggests jobs in web design and web administration may be quite secure in the future. Clearly, posting the latest promotional and stock information to maintain current custom and attract new customers will always be important. Online shopping rose by 40 per cent in 2006, with 2007 adding an extra £4 billion to the online shopping bill. This clearly demonstrates that retailers who ignore online shopping do so at their peril.

FASCINATING FACT

The worldwide market for PCs grew 12 per cent in the first quarter of 2008, which equals 71.1 million units and is an increase of 12.3 per cent on the same period in 2007.
Source: Anthony Savaas, *Computer Weekly*.

ENGINEERING AND SCIENCE

Technology plays a crucial role in any engineering or science-based industry with hybrid computers and specialist software used to number-crunch, manufacture, record and analyse vast amounts of data. This sector plays a significant role in creating innovative solutions and products which drive many of the new web-based technologies mentioned earlier in this chapter. The internet itself is a vital research and professional networking tool for scientists and engineers, but this sector also incorporates computer engineers and computer scientists at the sharp end of one of the greatest challengers of our time – internet security!

CHAPTER 2

Internet roles at a glance

The internet has to be one of the most uncertain and yet hugely exciting career areas to enter. As we have already discovered, there is very little actual data on specific employment trends for internet-related occupations. Yet, fewer careers could boast so many newly created opportunities and job roles. Before we explore these different roles in greater detail in Chapter 3 – and following complementary chapters on skills and qualities, training and qualifications – we will discover that specific web-based careers span a number of significant and distinctive occupational sectors. They are also at the forefront of creative, technical and commercial innovation. With this comes an increased amount of uncertainty as technology continually shifts, influences and redefines job roles for the future, but the personal and financial rewards can be very enticing particularly if you are prepared to manage and up-skill your own career portfolio.

WHAT'S IN A NAME?

As might be expected, any names and roles describing internet-related careers suffer, like their IT relatives, from a vast array of overlapping and confusing job titles. For example, a web controller, web developer and web infrastructure engineer could all be one and the same job. Is a web designer the same as a graphic designer, or an online publicist a web advertiser?

Firstly, to help explain some of the confusion as well as introduce the many different job roles, we have taken a little creative licence by selecting four specific internet job roles with shared main functions and skill requirements (see Figure 1: internet at-a-glance chart). This should be particularly useful if you know you want to work with the internet but are uncertain about the type of role or specific sector to join. Secondly, each role is then introduced in more detail, including, wherever possible, average salaries as well as positive and negative aspects of the work and future prospects. Do note that while some jobs will include similar skill elements, other organisations might employ specialists from all four skill sets covered on page 19.

FIGURE 1: INTERNET AT-A-GLANCE CHART

How it works (technical and scientific)

Web developer – *also known as or has some shared skill requirements with*:

Web infrastructure engineer
Web controller/webmaster/
  web manager
Web account director
Web applications developer
Internet security specialist
Search engine optimisation
  specialist

Internet/web programmer
Web infrastructure support
  analyst
Internet/web professional
Web administrator
Web tester

How it works (design and audiovisual)

Web designer – *also known as or has some shared skill requirements with*:

Internet designer
Graphic designer
  (with programming)
Multimedia specialist
Computer games designer

Web architect
Web and user interface
  designer
Interactive media designer

How it feels (content and information)

Web content manager – *also known as or has some shared skill requirements with*:

Website editor/author
Website publicist
E-learning developer/
  technologist
Database operator/data enterer

Internet writer/journalist
Online publisher
Database administrator

How it sells (commercial and marketing)

Online marketing consultant – *also known as or has some shared skill requirements with*:

E-commerce development
  manager
Online sales/account
  manager
E-commerce analyst

Head of e-commerce
Marketing officer
  (e-communications)

CHAPTER 3

Technical and scientific roles

If someone asked you how the internet works would your reaction be 'It's beyond me!' or something similar, or would you almost instinctively be interested, or want to understand something of its technical complexity and its synergetic power to transform and globalise information technology? If, more specifically, you are naturally excited about working with the internet and related applications, then this chapter should help you examine some of the most common technical and scientific job roles. We will begin by exploring the work of a web developer, the skills and qualities you may need, negative and positive aspects of work, average salaries and your employment prospects. We will also complement our understanding of the technical landscape by adding a number of jargon buster explanations and a highly informative personal case study.

WEB DEVELOPER

As a web developer you could be using your technical and programming experience towards developing and implementing your organisation's web-based services. Depending on the size of the organisation, you may lead or be part of a wider creative and support team offering integrated solutions to meet internal colleague (intranet/extranet) as well as client and customer needs. You will also be required to keep right up to date with advancing technologies, testing and security developments. It is possible that you might inform company strategy on training, or possibly deliver internal staff training courses yourself. In smaller organisations, your role might include elements of web design (see Chapter 4).

POSITIVE AND NEGATIVE ASPECTS

Successful web developers can take a great deal of credit as more and more private and public organisations become extremely reliant upon their website(s) to market, sell or inform on their core business. The policies you implement could significantly influence increased 'site traffic' and income to your company. Also, being part of a creative team and continually troubleshooting technical problems can be very challenging, but rewarding too. However, on the downside, you might be faced with irate colleagues or customers who don't appreciate the difficulties when certain technical concerns take time to sort out and, in some organisations, you might find yourself frustrated by having to work constantly to unrealistic timescales and deadlines can be very frustrating.

PROSPECTS

Because web developers work across most organisations and different industrial sectors, it is likely that your prospects for professional development are very good. From 2004–2008 there was an increase of 3–4.5 per cent in web developer vacancies. This is likely to grow further with new support functions underpinning the integration of online and offline applications. As you become more experienced and qualified as a web developer, there may well be opportunities to be self-employed and to offer a range of consultancy services.

AVERAGE SALARIES

Average salaries start at £20 000–£29 000, but, when fully experienced, you could earn between £30 000 and £39 000 with as high as £69 000 per year. Contract workers can earn short term, but equally high salaries. Please note that average salaries are typical across the range of job roles outlined.

SIMILAR OR SHARED JOB ROLES AND SKILLS, BUT ARE THERE ANY DIFFERENCES?

As seen from the at-a-glance chart on page 19, web controllers can share similar or the same technical and scientific skills with other related job roles. In some cases they might perform exactly the same requirements as a job advertised under a different name! To help with this confusion we have included below the job roles which are most closely related in functional skills, but also briefly commented where possible variances occur. Do check out the recommended job-hunting agencies mentioned in Chapter 9. It is by comparing these specific job functions with your own skills that you can identify your interest or suitability for a given job role.

FASCINATING FACT

Internet addiction is becoming a more common compulsive disorder according to Dr Block at the University of Portland USA. See http://ajp.psychiatryonline.org.

WEB INFRASTRUCTURE ENGINEER

As a web infrastructure engineer you might well have a specific responsibility within your company for the monitoring, trouble-shooting and performance management of mission critical servers. Your advanced technical and programming skills could be used to develop the next generation of web service APIs (application program interfaces) and implement services, servers and appropriate infrastructure to process to a successful outcome.

WEB INFRASTRUCTURE SUPPORT ANALYST

A web infrastructure support analyst's responsibilities include support and maintenance of internal infrastructure including web servers, wireless network, VPN (virtual private networking), Windows and Linux operating systems. You are likely to log support calls from customers as well as resolving any initial issues and part of your regular role will be to carry out application functional and performance testing of your organisation's web-based and software systems.

INTERNET/WEB PROGRAMMER OR PROFESSIONAL

The skills you have as an internet programmer or web professional will be utilised by most small, medium and large-scale organisations. However, it is possible after gaining suitable experience to work independently as a consultant where you are brought in to troubleshoot particular problems or introduce a range of web-based solutions and services.

WEB ACCOUNT DIRECTOR/PROJECT MANAGER

Web account directors essentially have a co-ordinating role over a wide range of different projects. This can include responsibility for the more sophisticated websites offering web hosting, handling online enquiries, overseeing sales and payment systems and maximising search engine optimisation (SEO) to create further business opportunities.

WEB APPLICATIONS DEVELOPER

As a web applications developer you could be deciding the most economical and powerful choice of platform for large multi-user systems. In the past, software had to be distributed and physically installed onto potentially thousands of client computers, but today's web applications developers implement business-critical database applications. This could include online retail sales, online auctions, wikis, discussion boards, weblogs and many other functions.

INTERNET SECURITY ANALYST/CO-ORDINATOR

Internet security (IS) analysts are increasingly at the frontline of troubleshooting problems and faults. This includes planning and implementing security measures to protect clients' information and data from unauthorised access, deliberate attack, theft and corruption. Security analysts also put controls in place to allow the secure transfer of files and data across computer networks. Your role will also include simulating breaches to test procedures (known as penetration testing), investigating actual breaches and carrying out corrective actions as well as testing systems for weak points (known as vulnerability scanning).

Jargon Busters – Security

hacker   someone who breaks into secured systems and occasionally causes unparalleled harm to businesses or individual lives – hacking has been going on since computers were invented and sometimes there have been extremely damaging consequences. Some old-time hackers have now 'gone commercial' and taken hacking to the business level (referred to as 'ethical hackers').

virus/worm   software program that replicates itself on computer systems – can be harmless, displaying an annoying message, but can also destroy files or disable a computer altogether. Viruses tend to spread rapidly, particularly when transmitted via email; 'strains' have appeared that use personal email address books to propagate themselves from machine to machine. If you are connected to the internet or any other network, it is important that you take precautions against viruses. Get a virus-scanning program and do not open any email attachments from people you do not know.

spyware   software that gathers information about a user as he or she navigates around the web – intended to track surfing habits in order to build marketing profiles. Spyware is often included in 'free downloads' from the web, where the license agreement (which so many of us accept without reading) may mention that information about your habits will be transmitted back to the company's website. Spyware is a major cause for public concern about privacy on the internet.

phishing   online scam where seemingly legitimate emails encourage users to leave confidential details on spoof websites.

pharming   redirects users to fake websites by hijacking genuine website addresses – potential to 'capture' passwords and other data.

Trojan/Trojan horse   type of computer virus disguised as a program – the scenario usually happens like this: a user may download a program from the internet because they think it may be of some use; but once the program is opened (or run), it releases a virus that erases their hard drive or wreaks havoc on their system. One notorious Trojan horse virus came in the form of an email attachment of a file called AOL4FREE.COM, and the 'I Love You' virus is another example. The name comes from the Greek legend of a wooden horse that looks harmless, but actually harbours trouble.

Many of the above jargon busters have been reproduced by permission of © 1994–2008 NetLingo™ The Internet Dictionary at http://www.netlingo.com.

SEARCH ENGINE OPTIMISATION SPECIALIST, SEARCH ENGINE ANALYST

Your main role as a specialist in search engine optimisation is to track, maintain and analyse the traffic from search engines to your organisation's website. This will include establishing and monitoring good practices such as keyword ranking, indexed pages and back links. You will communicate progress to stakeholders and provide answers to their questions. You will also be involved in researching new initiatives to improve SEO wherever possible. The role, while varied and interesting, is likely to be quite demanding particularly if you are working within a highly competitive market where you are expected to stimulate high levels of volume and good quality of traffic to your site.

WEB TESTER

As we have seen, web testing forms part of many internet jobs in this technical and scientific range, however, some organisations could employ you specifically in this role. Your responsibilities are likely to include testing for design and accessibility, such as alternative views for JavaScript and mobile devices, as well as website consistency in resolution and colour. Then there are a host of specific test requirements, such as cache, compatibility, cookie, default, form, functionality and much more (as outlined in the next jargon buster).

Jargon Buster – Web Tester

Listed below are brief descriptions of more internet terms which also form just a sample of the functions, software and programs a web tester could be responsible for. Others include: alternative views, boundary testing, consistency of design, default settings, display settings, form controls, interruption of page loading, link testing, localisation testing, page content, performance testing, printing and resource utilisation.

accessibility involves making computer technology and internet resources useful to more people than would otherwise be the case. Internet accessibility attempts to allow the participation of people with disabilities. It can also include consideration for people whose communication infrastructures or capabilities are not advanced or not in place. Source: UN – www.un.org/esa/socdev/enable/disacc00.htm.

ActiveX a set of technologies created by Microsoft to enable interactive content on websites. With ActiveX, websites can be animated using multimedia effects, interactive objects, and sophisticated applications that create a user experience comparable to a high-quality CD-ROM.

cache testing action of storing web files for later reuse so that they can be accessed more quickly by the end user. When you're on the web, the cache improves your web browser's performance: it stores HTML page code, graphics, and multimedia elements so that when you return to that particular webpage (even if you just hit the back button), the information doesn't have to be downloaded all over again. There are procedures a web tester adopts to test these functions.

compatibility testing frequently used term referring to the ability of a hardware device or software program to work with another kind of device or program. For example, a user may try to substitute one brand (or model) of a computer for another and then try to run the same software on it; to be truly compatible, a program or device must operate on a given system without any changes. A web tester makes sure appropriate checks are carried out on a regular basis.

cookie testing   a funny name for a noun that describes a small piece of information about you (about your computer, actually). It is a small file that a web server automatically sends to your PC when you browse certain websites. Cookies are stored as text files on your hard drive so servers can access them when you return to websites you've visited before.

functionality   how something works or operates, or online, what purpose it serves. For example, a website that allows people to purchase an item online has a distinct functionality from one that simply lets users post and read other people's information. Functionality actually means the same as function, but for some reason it is referred to in the industry as the functionality.

Java   programming language developed by Sun Microsystems, specifically designed for writing programs that can be safely downloaded through the internet without fear of viruses or other harm to computers or files.

JavaScript   scripting language to enable webpage authors to design interactive sites. Although it shares many of the features and structures of the full Java language, it was developed independently. JavaScript can interact with HTML source code, enabling web developers to jazz up their sites with dynamic content.

multimedia content   computer-based method of presenting combinations of text, images, graphics, animation, streaming audio or video, and so on. 'Modern multimedia' features an emphasis on interactivity.

navigation   act of moving around the web by clicking on hypertext links (or paths) that take you from one page to another. As you navigate, you move from one computer to another and from one server to another without realising it.

search functions process of locating information on the internet, whether on a website, newsgroup, or in an archive. In order to do a search, users often begin at search engines, search directories, or portals.

security testing protection of data so that unauthorised users cannot access it or copy it. Security can mean anything from a screen saver with a password to encrypted data that cannot be read without the proper decoding software.

Reproduced by permission of © 1994–2008 NetLingo™ The Internet Dictionary *at http://www.netlingo.com.*

WEB ADMINISTRATOR

Within this section a web administrator has a largely technical rather than administrative function and is likely to be part of the web team customising, administering, deploying and supporting a number of web-based software applications. Tasks might include simple JavaScript programming as well as testing applications across multiple browser platforms. This can be an excellent first or second career move in preparation for entering further webpage development careers with increased responsibility.

FASCINATING FACT

Today, at any one moment, there are more than 50 million people using the internet. This makes it the biggest market place the civilised world has ever known.

SKILLS AND QUALITIES

Now that you have had the opportunity to look at the many different as well as interrelated technical and scientific job opportunities in the internet, we need to uncover and tease out whether you have the personal skills and qualities needed to do a particular type of work. Again there is some overlap so we have summarised common requirements from internet-based employers, as well as explored a selection of more specific requirements they might have. Later in this chapter we will look at Chris Hutchinson's case study, which is an invaluable source of information about the role of a web developer. He tells us what this particular job is really like and will help you identify whether you have the right personality and potential to make a success in a similar career. It is important not to be overwhelmed by the listings below. All employers will require the highest level abilities in specific areas, but none of us are superhuman! Also, some skills can only be gained by particular educational or employment experience, which we discuss further in Chapter 8.

WEB DEVELOPER

As a web developer your primary skill is to assess and analyse the technical needs of your organisation or customer and co-ordinate agreed delivery outcomes and solutions to deadlines and within budget. So, in no particular order and depending on the given organisation, you will need:

- considerable interest in technical and scientific web-based applications

- excellent people and time management skills

- good verbal and writing ability

- analytical and problem-solving skills

- attention to detail

- ability to solve complex problems in a logical manner

- up-to-date and broad knowledge of internet technologies

- project management skills for more senior roles or consultancy work

- excellent web and database programming skills

- costing and financial management skills

- good understanding and appreciation of design, usability and interactivity

- creative and imaginative ability to turn clients' ideas into workable plans

- willingness to work flexibly, part of a team or alone

- thorough knowledge of international web development standards.

RELATED OR ADDITIONAL SKILL NEEDS
Web infrastructure engineer
If you are working for an ISP you are likely to need:

- advanced critical analysis, technical and programming skills.

Web infrastructure support analyst
Working in support and maintenance of a variety of operating systems you are likely to need:

- organisational and record management abilities.

Web Administrator
Sample of employer requirements

Web administrator with solid knowledge of J2EE products. Suitable candidates will need to have solid web technologies and e-commerce-related technologies skills coupled with knowledge of working with application servers (Websphere/ Tomcat), Java, JSP and web servers (iPlanet, IIS, IHS).

Web Application Support/Systems Administrator
Sample of employer requirements

Ideally web logic and Unix (preferably Solaris) skills are required. Also, SQL, Perl and Apache web server experience. Duties will involve full technical management of the web application, systems administration and web server patch maintenance, security control, bug tracking and investigation.

IS analysts/co-ordinators
IS analysts will require particular abilities to:

- interpret and evaluate data

- understand confidentiality issues

- be committed to keeping up to date with emerging security threats, technologies and trends

- possess knowledge of information security standards and legislation.

IS Co-ordinator
Sample of employer requirements

Experience of different operating and server systems, such as Windows, Unix and Linux, and security technologies and procedures, such as firewalls and anti-virus software, intrusion detection systems (IDS), encryption techniques, such as Public Key Infrastructure (PKI) and Secure Socket Layer (SSL) authentication (passwords, digital certificates and, more recently, biometrics), penetration testing and vulnerability scanning. Be willing to undertake further training and industry-recognised certifications.

SEO consultant
Sample of employer requirements

Knowledge of internet, strong client-facing skills and web development technologies: HTML, XHTML, Java, CSS, Flash, ASP and PHP will be essential. Other helpful technical skills include administration experience of UNIX, Apache, DNS, log files as well as appreciation of CMS and dynamic URs, and web analytics and techniques. Working knowledge of programming in Coldfusion, Perl, ASP, PHP with XML and RSS would be beneficial.

SEO specialist/search engine analyst
This specialist role will require:

- excellent knowledge of the search engine marketing industry

- passion and drive to excel in this fast-paced environment.

Case Study 1
Chris Hutchinson – Web Developer

How did you get your first job – and what was it?
My first part-time job was as a till operator/customer service assistant at Tesco. Like a lot of my friends at the time, we took on part-time jobs during college to help pay for everyday living and, of course, for fun! Since then I have had many different jobs. I spent a gap year between college and university working as a voluntary instructor at an outdoor education centre in Wales; I worked as an events and PR co-ordinator at Westland Helicopters in Somerset; I then spent a long period of time working at Portsmouth City Council, starting as a housing benefit officer and then moving into internal communications and, finally, into my first official

job doing what I do now, as the intranet project co-ordinator. Although the jobs I have done are varied, a common theme throughout has been the use of internet technologies to facilitate my everyday tasks or to achieve goals. For example, I created a promotional website for the outdoor education centre, I used web technology to produce interactive CD-ROMs at Westland Helicopters and used my skills to develop an intranet when working within internal communications. Since leaving the council, I have set up my own web development business full time.

What has helped you to progress?

Over the course of my career to date, I think the thing that has helped me most is keeping an interest in what I have been doing and always looking forward. I have found myself in roles that were not particularly interesting or stimulating, however, if you try and understand exactly what it is that you don't like about a job, you can use this information to help identify roles that you might enjoy more. It's often easier to identify what you don't like doing rather than trying to find the one job that you are completely suited to. In the majority of roles I have been in, I have found that there were often ways you could use your own interests and skills in the workplace to do additional tasks that help make your working life more varied and interesting. Finally, although it's not always easy, I've tried to keep one eye open to the next opportunity and tried never to take the easy route just because it is easy! Having the confidence to leave a relatively well-paid job and set up business on my own was a big step. However, by taking the time to work everything out, including working out incomings and outgoings, I was able to minimise the risks associated with taking a step like this. Remaining confident in my abilities and thinking of things as adventures helps as well.

Do you think your educational background was helpful preparation and if so how?

Although my education and the subjects I chose didn't directly relate to my role as a web developer, there's no doubt that the skills and knowledge I picked up through school were incredibly useful: from problem-solving skills, to writing essays and more general skills. I think something that is overlooked when thinking about school and education are the skills you are picking up outside of the actual subjects you are learning. School, college and university are just as much about learning how to get on with your peers, establishing relationships and learning to work in teams and college and university are a great help in learning to become independent. Finally, although in my mind it's not the most important aspect of education, gaining good qualifications will help when applying for jobs. Not just based on the actual results attained, but as much because gaining qualifications shows that you work hard and can take an interest.

Can you summarise a typical working day?
For some of the jobs I've had it would be easy to quickly write down all the things I might do in a typical day. However, it's a bit more difficult for my current job running my own small company that specialises in web development. I work from home at the moment, which means I only have a five-metre commute to the office! I know plenty of people who say they couldn't cope with the discipline of making sure they got out of bed on time every day! I haven't had a problem with this at all, but I do certainly enjoy the flexibility of being able to work whenever and wherever I choose. I work incredibly closely with a good team of people. Even though my role is relatively wide, I need the support of others to enable me to do what I do. Working from home, I obviously don't have a team of people sat around me, however, I am constantly using the internet or phone and remain in close contact with my team, via email for example. I have a strong relationship with around five different web designers. These are graphical artists whom I work with to turn a client's requirements into an actual website. I am not a highly creative person so I use my designers' skills, as creative people, to come up with websites that not only look great, but also work well and make sense to users. A lot of my time is taken up with

actually carrying out the technical aspects of putting websites together. This means I spend a relatively long time in front of a computer. However, another important aspect of my role is to go out to visit clients and to pitch for new work. This involves presenting ideas and writing proposal documents. On top of these main aspects of my role, I also do a lot of everyday business tasks, like invoicing, banking and marketing.

One final important aspect of my day-to-day work is making sure that I am up to date with all the new technologies that are being used on the web. This can be as simple as surfing the web to see how people are using Facebook, or just looking at some clever ideas that people are working on. However, there's a serious side to this also, which is that I need to make sure that I have sufficient skills to keep up to speed with the industry I work in. A lot of my skills are self-taught, both from books but also from the internet. The internet is a great resource for people in my industry but it also moves at an incredible pace and so I have to pay careful attention to make sure I don't fall behind.

What are the best things and the worst things about your job?
I think the best and worst things about my job are perhaps exactly the same! Being in charge of my own working day and business means I'm free to do as I wish. I can decide to vary my working day however I choose and I could even wake up one day and decide to go in a completely different direction in life if that was what I wanted! The limiting factor is that I need to make sure that I remain earning enough money to pay for the absolute basics – e.g. house, food and bills. However, this also has a stressful side to it, as without the support and infrastructure of a large company sitting behind you, there is no guaranteed regular salary. If I work hard, have a lot of business directed my way and complete it all, I get paid. If I am ill or I have a couple of months where I don't get a lot of business, I don't get paid. This can obviously be worrying and stressful.

Have you any advice for school leavers wishing to enter a career as a web developer?

My route into being a web developer didn't really tie in directly with my education or my early jobs, however, making websites, being involved in design and generally using computer technologies have always been among my hobbies. I think having an interest in the work I have ended up doing has been a good thing. I don't just do a job because I can do it, I do it because I enjoy it.

I think that gaining qualifications in computing and programming would help someone wanting to do a similar role to me and having a good knowledge of how to use graphics packages (if not the creative skill to actually create anything good!) is really useful as well.

Although I didn't start out directly in the role I have ended up doing, keeping my eyes open to opportunities and maximising what you are learning from any role means that you create a rounded skill-set, and one which is far more useful to both employers and to yourself.

Can you identify any qualities that are likely to help someone succeed?

There are many ways to identify success. A lot of people put too much emphasis on how much someone earns as a sign of success. Earning money in life is important in some ways but I would recommend that you measure success in more ways than this. Therefore, to succeed, you should first try and identify what exactly you are looking for, or indeed are looking to avoid, in life. Then the qualities you need to achieve that are relatively universal. You need to set a plan or goals, you need to be disciplined enough to work towards those goals even when the going gets hard and you need to understand that not everything gets given to you on a plate. Some things you just need to go and get yourself.

What do you think the future holds for you and for the industry?

The industry I work in is evolving at an incredible rate. It's moved from being a fringe technology to the core of all mainstream business in only a few years. There is therefore a lot of pressure on people in my industry to supply technologies and services to everyone that were once complex and specialist. For me, that will involve making sure that my finger is always on the pulse as far as new technologies and opportunities go.

I'm always re-assessing my goals and working towards them, so who knows where I'll be or what I'll be doing in five years' time. All I know is that it will be an adventure along the way!

CHAPTER 4

Design and audiovisual roles

We live increasingly in a very sophisticated visual age where there is an expectation that everything must look interesting and attractive in order to grab our attention. As we are about to discover, this is particularly relevant to the work of web designers. In this chapter, we will look at their job role in some detail including negative and positive aspects, salaries and prospects as well as skills and qualities that suit this type of work. We will also see how a number of related careers in multimedia and interface design are impacting on designers' work and conclude with an inspiring case study from a recent interactive media student.

WEB DESIGNER

Web designers often provide that essential creative inspiration that also acts as a catalyst to an organisation's development and improved success. However, few jobs have been as influenced and challenged more by the development of interactive web-based technologies. It seems that if graphic designers are to make the crossover to web design then they will need a whole new set of creative and technical abilities. The traditional skills and training requirements may be similar to what was needed in the past, but the end product or service, the way your designs are visualised and interacted with in a web-based environment, could be very different. Also, your designs may have to complement and integrate with a range of other media including film and sound clips, live newsfeeds, podcasts etc. You will be required to keep right up to date with advancing technologies and an increasing range of delivery platforms. Your designs might be viewed on a small mobile phone or mini–PC or on multi-screen devices and new home screen applications. So, working well in a team with other colleagues, such as web controllers and ultimately end users, will be an important aspect of your role.

POSITIVE AND NEGATIVE ASPECTS
Variety is a very appealing aspect of a web designer's work. You may be involved in a wide range of projects, for example designing interactive educational resources, or an online shopping facility, a downloadable conference brochure or a training document. Your work may be widely appreciated by colleagues in the same building or by customers on the other side of the world. Like any job, though, there are aspects that may not be so appealing, such as meeting clients to discuss their requirements or working within fixed time constraints or a given budget. There is nothing better than stimulating a 'Wow!' reaction to your work, but you also have to be thick-skinned if colleagues or clients occasionally don't respond well to your masterpieces!

PROSPECTS
These are nothing short of excellent as long as you are prepared to go where the work is available and, if necessary, move companies to keep your skills up to date. These days almost every small to large organisation, charity and service requires a web presence. While some online web design services have their place and related software integration will become easier with 'pick and mix' ready programs, the unique skills and qualities of providing original designs will always be appreciated. There are also increasing opportunities to work remotely, be self-employed and to offer a range of consultancy services.

AVERAGE SALARIES

Salaries for new web designers can range between £15 000 and £20 000 a year with experienced designers earning up to £30 000. Senior designers and those with specialist programming skills may earn up to £40 000. Self-employed web designers negotiate their own rates.

As a web designer and particularly as a web controller/developer you are likely to meet colleagues or customers on a regular basis. Below is a list of sample questions you might have to ask and then, crucially, deliver on.

WHAT KIND OF PROJECT IS BEING UNDERTAKEN?

- for a new or existing company

- totally new project

- development of an existing service

WHAT TIMESCALES AND COMMITMENT DEADLINES ARE THERE?

- key milestone development phases

- date when site goes live and how time critical is this deadline

WHAT FUNCTIONALITY IS REQUIRED?

- content management system (permits site editing)

- e-commerce facility for selling products and services

- types of drop-down menus and listings

- online forms

- any media and interactivity, such as multimedia, film, podcasting or RSS news services

- edited forum discussion facilities

- customer service support options

WHAT WEB-BASED LANGUAGE DO YOU REQUIRE?

● examples: Microsoft .NET, ASP, Java, Open Source FOSS, PHP, Perl or other

See jargon buster 'Languages' on page 92 for a brief explanation.

SIMILAR OR SHARED JOB ROLES AND SKILLS, BUT ARE THERE ANY DIFFERENCES?

As seen from the at-a-glance comparison chart (on page 19), web designers can share similar or the same design and audiovisual skills with other related job roles. In some cases, they might perform exactly the same requirements as a job advertised under a different name! To help with this confusion we have included below the job roles which are most closely related to web design in functional skills, but also we have briefly commented where possible variances occur. Do check out the recommended job-hunting agencies mentioned in Chapter 9. It is by comparing these specific job functions with your own skills that you can identify your interest or suitability for a given job role.

WEB ARCHITECT

This term seems to be used by a number of companies to describe the overall service they provide and less about a given job role. The emphasis on supplying standard compliant web infrastructure to any given project is key, with an overlap between web design and web developer roles. In the US some web designers are referred to as web architects. However, the University of Greenwich MA in web design and content planning defines website architecture as 'the art and science of creating good websites'. It describes a broad approach to planning and design, calling it architecture because, like physical architecture, it embraces engineering, aesthetic and usability aspects.

GRAPHIC DESIGNER (WITH PROGRAMMING)

This role is likely to be identical to the that of a web designer described earlier and emphasises the evolving nature of this sector, which requires individuals to meet new expectations and develop additional related skills.

WEB AND USER INTERFACE DESIGNER

As a web and user interface designer, you are likely to be at the forefront of all aspects of integrating web and digital-based technologies. As we have already mentioned, the PC is just one of an extensive range of devices used in the workplace including mobile phones, personal organisers, web-conferencing facilities etc. This suggests that a more technical role will be involved where Web 2 applications are necessary. However, some job descriptions also emphasise using design skills to upgrade a company's existing materials and resources into a digital and web-based environment. This offers the potential for colleagues to work remotely and call up any given resource, graphic, sound, file or photo image in an instant.

MULTIMEDIA SPECIALIST/INTERACTIVE MEDIA DESIGNER

In this role, you will be creating the overall feel and visual presentation of a wide range of interactive communication services and products. You may be working and applying text, data, graphics, sound, animation and other digital and visual effects, into given websites, online/offline games, virtual learning environments and other media. Much depends on the type of public or private organisation that employs you, but as an interactive media designer you could be working alongside specialist writers, animators, programmers and be applying industry-standard specialised graphics and multimedia software packages. Designers often work for graphic design, advertising or marketing and communications agencies.

COMPUTER GAMES DESIGNER

As a computer games designer you will be using your considerable creative skills and ability to create storyboards and flowcharts in support of managing all aspects of the playing experience. You will work within a team of creative people who will produce anything from scripts to programming, animation to sound effects and music. It is clear from current and likely future trends that most of the main games makers are moving over towards providing their games within an online and multi-interface environment. How long might it be before some of the best and most popular games are shared within a given social network site?

SKILLS AND QUALITIES

WEB DESIGNER

Web designers are at the forefront of the current technological revolution. Their exceptional, natural and creative abilities to visualise and produce unique designs to suit a web audience will benefit from being supplemented by many of the following characteristics:

- You enjoy the challenge of turning other people's ideas and concepts into visual messages.

- You like meeting clients and discussing creative solutions.

- You can work alone or with a team.

- You are good at explaining technical web design issues in understandable layperson's terms.

- You enjoy problem-solving and using a logical approach to tasks.

- You are able to prepare a clear design plan, presenting site structure and showing how different parts interact online.

- You have a flair for selecting text styles, colours and background images.

- You enjoy using design software to layout pages, positioning buttons, links and pictures.

- You can work with multimedia features such as sound, animation and video.

- You are interested in internet programming and able to pick up new techniques.

- You can test and refine design and site features.

- You can work to deadlines and within budget constraints.

- You have a knowledge of legislation and guidelines for website accessibility.

- You enjoy keeping up to date on changes in technology and software.

- You possess business management and negotiating skills – particularly if hoping to be self-employed.

Web/User Interface Designer
Sample of employer requirements

Internet Application and User interface experience including dynamic personalisation technologies and cross-channel applications (mobile, web, call centre, retail environments etc.) Good hand coder of HTML, XHTML and CSS essential. Software packages experience: Adobe Dreamweaver, Photoshop, Illustrator, InDesign, Flash. Understanding of W3C, WAI standards and basic knowledge of SQL and PHP. Knowledge of SEO and web marketing.

See the jargon buster on page 92 for most of the technical names listed above.

RELATED OR ADDITIONAL SKILL NEEDS

WEB ARCHITECT
If you are web architect you are likely to require particular abilities in:

- attention to technical compliancy requirements.

WEB AND USER INTERFACE DESIGNER
As a web or user interface designer you will benefit from having the following additional skills or interests:

- passion for new and evolving technology platforms and devices for delivering information

- desire to provide digital and web-based solutions to complex problems

- keen interest in enhancing user experience and making appropriate improvements

- ability to create and maintain good levels of business documentation.

MULTIMEDIA SPECIALIST/INTERACTIVE MEDIA DESIGNER

Multimedia specialists and interactive media designers will have abilities which include:

- interest in the future of interactive media, particularly digital technology

- enjoyment of the challenges of working across many different media

- knowledge of computer technology and the technical processes involved.

GAMES DESIGNER

As a games designer working increasingly with web-based media you will be:

- passionate for games playing, with the ability to play at high levels

- able to recognise the importance of working with other creative individuals on a project

- patient and persevering with detailed and repetitive work

- knowledgeable about the games market

- respectful and tactful with colleagues who might not agree with your suggestions.

See Chapter 9 'Next Steps and Resources' (page 102) for further information.

As we you will see in Chapter 8, there are many different routes into training for web design ranging from Level 2–3 qualifications (mainly college/employer) through to Level 4–5 (undergraduate and postgraduate) courses. However, if this is already of great interest to you, what better place to start than from the real-life experiences of a recent graduate?

Case Study 2
Simon English – Web Designer with Whitlelight Creative

How did you get your first job – and what was it?
To define my first job as a web designer would be a very difficult thing to do. Part of my progression is owed to my urge to dabble and experiment with small design tasks from a very young age, purely to develop skills and develop artistic sensibilities. I think all successful designers in industry can trace back personality traits and habits to a very young age that indicated that they may have had the potential to develop such skills and mindset.

However, if I was to define my first paid job it would have been for a small Guernsey-based 3D animation specialist. I worked at this point alone as a freelancer, full of excitement and enthusiasm for the situation but naïve to the complications and necessity of efficient communication and, that horrible word, compromise that are all too familiar to hard-nosed designers/businesspeople across the country.

Like many developing designers, I was at university at this stage studying interactive media, the course and my tutors began to give me the confidence that, despite a young age and lack of business acumen, web design is an industry that allows freelancers/individuals to undertake work without too much logistical and financial constraint: this limited demand for infrastructure is in itself one of the most appealing aspects about the industry for any young designer.

I sourced the job by keeping my ear to the ground at all times and jumping at any chance to undertake work, paid or not at this point. Having a strong portfolio was also a great advantage.

What has helped you to progress?
Before I can answer this, I need to consider the context of the question. To progress in skills, career or thinking? There are many factors that aid the development of all these areas, some obvious and some that only come to light years after their conception. Education is something that has a marked effect on all of these areas, but I will save that for the next question.

A designer's skill-set, program knowledge and application is something that is continuously being developed. I think for these attributes to develop they need to be challenged. To dabble in design for its own sake can help, but to be challenged and for skills to commercially progress you must undertake tasks that are either unfamiliar, out of your comfort zone or on behalf of a critical audience. Whether that audience is a paying customer, a university lecturer or your peers is not as important. It is this external pressure that will drive you to succeed and gain gratification from your exploits.

I think that for your thinking to progress, you must be critiqued, thus educating yourself in how to perform a critique and analysis of your own work and others'. This encourages aesthetic awareness and develops a natural tendency to refine any output. This ability/tendency to perform critical analysis of written text, designs and opinion, wherever sourced and digested, allows designers to learn far more from everything around them. Blogs form a great basis for discussion and allow designers to return to their comments at any time to augment both visual and textual elements, thus provoking reaction from the community around them. Learning and benefiting from the designers around you in this way is one of the most marked factors affecting your progression.

Do you think your educational background was helpful preparation and if so how?

- A levels: media studies, IT
- Degree: interactive media, University of Portsmouth.

If we consider the educational background noted above, it would appear that there has been a logical progression to my job as a web designer. I think, however, that educational backgrounds often only reflect the wants and needs of a society. This is not to say that my education has not been insightful, but I would argue that it was not fundamental in developing my design skills. Pressures and expectations from government and employers often corner creative individuals into jumping through hoops to ensure they tick the right boxes and appear employable.

I would advise creative individuals to be aware of this but not become despondent. Although there are many people out there with design skills, many of them are not professional designers. This observation indicates that a strong and logical educational route, when well considered, can open many doors for individuals and provides numerous opportunities along their career path. Do not assume education is your ticket to your design job, but be aware that it will make available many more opportunities to live up to your potential.

Can you summarise a typical working day?
Before I summarise my working day, it is important to consider my situation. I am a self-employed web designer with a small business, comprising myself as designer and one developer who also works externally for other design firms.

1. Get up at my own pace and begin to take stock of the day's requirements

2. Get to work, either at home or at an office

3. Turn on my link to the world from which I've been detached for some time now (at least I hope) and open up Photoshop

4. Look at my job board – an enormous help to any designer

5. Contact/chase those enormously frustrating clients who
    just don't seem to understand the need for efficient
    communication

6. Work on my own pet projects, before my sensible side
    begins to realise that I need to finish some client work
    to put food on my table and pay my rapidly increasing
    electricity bills

7. I spend a lot of time drinking coffee and amending the
    mistakes of my developer post-wireframing of my PSDs.
    Once he's driven me to insanity and vice versa I grab
    my laptop and run down to the local coffee shop and
    keep working. The relationship between designer and
    developer is like a marriage, it requires patience,
    compromise, good communication and sometimes some
    space!

8. Work hard until things just stop flowing, any designer
    knows how it feels to just lose that get up and go.
    Sometimes that takes me through to 11p.m. without a
    blink and others I end up on my surfboard by 3p.m. in
    the afternoon

9. REPEAT!

What are the best things ... ?
I think the lack of logical timescale highlights a really nice
aspect of my job. I am my own master and my days are mine
to treat, in principal, how I wish. The average office job
requires an eight-hour stint of work from 9a.m.–5p.m. every
day. Whether I satisfy this quota and at what time in a
24-hour period is down to me and my conscience.

Flexibility is another great aspect. Due to increasingly
portable communications technologies designers are able to
work on the move day or night and anywhere across the globe
in a real-time environment that does not need to affect the
way they do their work or their client's needs.

The changeable demands of the job are what I relish. Every client or job is different, and the wants and needs of these new situations are always an exciting challenge to accommodate. To this avail I get to meet many new people, work with a variety of interesting media and travel all over the place to communicate with them and gather my own physical content.

I love reading and research, working on new briefs often provides an excuse to pick up a book and learn, to gain some historical and theoretical grounding on audiences and approach every situation form an enlightened perspective.

... and the worst things about your job?
Inconsistency of earnings can be a frustrating factor if self-employed. Sometimes you'll find yourself with an overwhelming amount of jobs and clients and other times you're fishing around your little black book of contacts chasing up old leads.

Slow clients – clients with an apparent lack of urgency to provide you what you need to finish the product they have employed you to create is the worst thing about the job whether self-employed or not. If you encounter this situation – which you will – you will need to refine the way you communicate with your clients otherwise, especially when self-employed, it will add to the financial pressure.

An inconsistent lifestyle and pressure of many expectant clients can be very stressful, but don't let that put you off; this I'm sure is true of any self-employed career path.

Have you any advice for school leavers wishing to enter a career as a web designer?
If you haven't had an interest in design until you leave school it's probably a strong indication that it's not for you. Most successful designers have enjoyed playing with what they do from a young age and in their spare time. If that's you and you love what you do, which you will need to, think long and hard about the benefits of choosing the right university course or

job placement. Choosing the wrong job or university course could damage your enthusiasm for your subject. Consider the aspects of what you do that you enjoy the most. We all use Photoshop, but is it the inception of work and communication, the development and research of ideas, or producing the work or the finished product that you relish? Let the answers to this self-analysis form the basis for an informed choice to come.

Life is full of choices so make sure you choose what's right for you and your developing talents, not what is expected of you by those around you or what you perceive society expects from you to succeed. Our industry is becoming increasingly specialised so don't be afraid to stick to what you are really good at, you'll never know everything!

Can you identify any qualities that are likely to help someone succeed?

- determination

- blind enthusiasm

- pixel perfection

- pride in your work

- strong, well-documented portfolio

- consideration of web design in other commercial circles: who affects you and whom do you affect?

- awareness (don't assume everything you learn is useful, be selective and intelligent about your choices).

What do you think the future holds for your industry?
For the designer, many things. The key thing to consider is that we are entering an information age. One must consider that information – and its collation – is becoming a product in itself. To this avail the job of a designer will

evolve and one must be far more informed culturally to cut it in our industry.

I think that designers will need to become far more adaptable to different media. Portable devices and the concept of the screen are constantly transforming and so, too, do the logistical constraints of size, speed and aesthetics.

What is real? Designers should all consider this question with regard to their work and the future of our society as new media technologies affect it and the way we live our lives, communicate and do business. As a result, globalisation will ultimately affect our industry and others. All designers have a serious responsibility to consider the effect of their products, cultural/artistic works and other outputs on those around them, as their reach is increasing rapidly.

I expect there will be a big backlash from consumers over information ownership, privacy and the link of new media to politics and global culture, as ignorant users begin to catch on to the effect of the technologies they have been utilising day to day for a large portion of their lives.

CHAPTER 5

Content and information roles

It is possible for an organisation to have the most attractively designed fully interactive website with wide-ranging multimedia functionality, but totally miss its purpose for existence and target audience. On the other hand, a site that is intuitive and almost second guesses its visitors' particular needs can inspire, motivate and generally enrich the user's web experience. In this chapter, we will discover this is particularly important to the work of web content managers. We will look at their job role in some detail including negative and positive aspects, salaries and prospects as well as the skills and qualities that suit this and other related types of work.

WEB CONTENT MANAGER

As a web content manager your increasingly specialist role is to create interest and build confidence in and loyalty to the information you are providing within your website. Depending on the size and type of your organisation you may be responsible for an editorial team who research and produce material including text, image and sound, or film media. In smaller organisations it is likely to be a more hands-on role with aspects of content production or service. In either role and depending on the complexity of the site, it is possible that you will have access to various content management and 'real time' programmes, so materials can be uploaded in an instant. As a web content manager your responsibilities may vary considerably from providing vital up-to-date public service information to your local community or local authority website to meeting business resource needs via an extranet service to colleagues in other parts of the UK or world.

POSITIVE AND NEGATIVE ASPECTS

A successful web content manager can feel a great sense of personal job satisfaction. Your mediating influence could play a vital role in an organisation's success. Detailed statistical reports can provide a direct correlation with the work you have co-ordinated and implemented to a resultant significant increase in traffic and possibly sales from your site. As a skilled organiser and editor, you can be a certain buzz to inspiring a dedicated team of creative and experienced individuals regularly to produce high quality work. On the downside, the role can be highly pressurised with deadlines and targets to meet, as well as widely different expectations and constant technological developments to keep up to date with.

PROSPECTS

Your prospects as a web content manager are excellent, although much depends on the size and type of organisation you work for. Options could include information management, technical web development and wider information planning and policy roles. It's interesting that traditional information and library roles within some organisations have developed into almost full-time web editing and content responsibilities; itself a form of progression. As you become more experienced, there may be opportunities for self-employment and offering consultancy services, but this will depend on your given area of expertise.

AVERAGE SALARIES

Salaries for web content managers can range between £25 000 and £50 000 a year depending on experience and seniority.

SIMILAR OR SHARED JOB ROLES AND SKILLS, BUT ARE THERE ANY DIFFERENCES?

As seen from the at-a-glance comparison chart (on page 19), web content managers can share similar or the same content and information skills with other related job roles. In some cases they might perform exactly the same requirements as a job advertised under a different name! To help with this confusion we have included below the job roles which are most closely related in functional skills, but also briefly commented where possible variances occur. Do check out the recommended job-hunting agencies mentioned in Chapter 9. It is by comparing these specific job functions with your own skills that you can identify your interest or suitability for a given job role.

WEBSITE EDITOR/AUTHOR

As a website editor your role will be to research, write, check and present text for your website's target audience. This can also include providing and editing multimedia content such as images, music, video and increasingly RSS newsfeeds. Your role may also be to upload materials using a content management system, making sure content is kept up to date, supporting online message boards and dealing with email enquiries. You might also attend planning and content commissioning meetings with other departments or clients, working closely with web developers, designers, public relations and marketing colleagues.

INTERNET WRITER/JOURNALIST

As an internet writer or journalist your role is likely to be in media-related industries with responsibility for writing articles, news features, press releases and other content for a web audience. With unprecedented growth in online readership, traditional journalists are increasingly making the leap to online and special transitional training is now available. As an internet journalist, a particular feature article you have written might well have linked audio or film with archive material or other related information.

WEBSITE PUBLICIST

Currently there are few roles advertised as a professional web or internet site publicist, but with the quality of websites improving significantly so too is the competition to maximise market share, or promote an organisation's website more effectively. Currently this may be a role shared within a web or information development team where content as well as design are seen as crucial. However, as an internet publicist you are likely to be involved particularly in developing appropriate web publicity plans, writing and editing email pitch materials and sending out review copy mailings. Also, writing and editing monthly e-newsletters, securing placement in web media, including social networking websites and blogs. (See also 'Online marketing manager' in Chapter 6 (page 64) below.)

E-LEARNING DEVELOPER/TECHNOLOGIST

A significant industry has grown up around web-based training, particularly corporate training where technology is used primarily to deliver content to the end user without significant interaction with (or support from) training professionals, peers or managers. As an e-learning developer you will build online training areas, known in the education world as virtual learning environments (VLE). VLEs are normally made up of course materials, email facilities, resources, and interactive coursework areas. A good example of this working in practice can be found on page 86 with the case study by Chris Wallace, who is undertaking a certified internet webmaster course with the Open University.

ONLINE PUBLISHER

As mentioned in the introduction, opportunities for self-publishing as well as B2B publishing are growing rapidly. In the commercial sector, you could work with trade journals, media-related industries, such as newspapers, magazines or broadcasting, where your skills as a researcher and editor of information will play a very important role.

DATABASE ADMINISTRATOR

As a database administrator you are likely to work for a medium to large-size organisation and be responsible for planning strategy, developing and maintaining computerised information systems, perhaps within the company's intranet or extranet services. Much depends on the type of business, but your role could also include linked telephony, populating data sets and a certain degree of site testing and repair.

DATABASE OPERATOR/DATA ENTERER

While traditionally the role of a database operator is common to most organisations – inputting data and updating records including text and figures – your role in this case will be interchanging data between an offline and online environment. Depending on the organisation you work for you might be allocating passwords and ensuring records are accurate, accessible and secure.

SKILLS AND QUALITIES

WEB CONTENT MANAGER

As a web content managers you will play a crucial role in co-ordinating all aspects of web information, media-related resources and design. Other skills and abilities required will depend on the type of websites you are responsible for but are likely to include some of the following characteristics:

- excellent organisational strengths

- ability to prioritise several tasks

- ability to work to deadlines

- understanding of legal issues, such as copyright, privacy and website accessibility

- good financial management ability and ability to work within budget

- negotiating and presentation skills

- excellent communication skills with colleagues and clients

- ability to encourage team-working skills

- appreciation of online writing issues, such as brevity, branding style, content and structure

- excellent grasp of English grammar, punctuation and spelling

- ability to write for a target audience

- attention to detail and proofreading.

RELATED OR ADDITIONAL SKILL NEEDS

WEBSITE EDITOR/AUTHOR/JOURNALIST

As a web editor/author you will have particular responsibility for written content on your website and so a number of other abilities and skills will be required, including:

- research and writing – being clear and concise and picking out important facts of information

- excellent understanding of English grammar, punctuation and spelling

- writing for a target audience

- creative ability in finding interesting ways of presenting web content.

E-LEARNING DEVELOPER

E-learning developers will have particular skill requirements depending on the type of learning resource they are responsible for. These may include:

- knowledge of web authoring and web development software

- passion for creative approaches to learning

- specialist teaching or lecturing experience

- excellent communication and co-ordinating skills

- ability to work with course tutors and programmers

- knowledge of further and higher education as well as business and commercial sectors.

WEBSITE PUBLICIST

As a website publicist you will be fully aware of website content and have a number of additional abilities and interests including:

- skill at organising campaign

- excellent planning and marketing skills

- thorough knowledge of all forms of e-communications

- ability to work with offline media

- knowledge of site optimisation techniques to improve search engine ranking

- writing press releases.

DATA ADMINISTRATOR

Data administrators are required to initiate and maintain accurate and effective office recording and information systems for both offline and increasingly online services, such as for extranet or main website platforms. Some of the specific abilities needed include:

- good communication and team-working skills

- enjoyment of problem-solving

- excellent organisational skills

- ability to work to a high degree of accuracy

- confidence in using a wide range of IT applications

- working well under pressure and to deadlines

- understanding of wider business demands

- good and sensitive staff negotiating skills

- appreciation of information laws, such as the Data Protection Act

- desire to keep up to date with developments in technology.

DATA OPERATORS

Data operators/data entry clerks will have a number of the skills and abilities above, but also:

- enjoy working in a busy office

- have essential numeracy and literacy skills

- good customer service abilities

- appreciate importance of confidential data

- can work quickly, accurately with attention to detail

- understanding of health and safety issues around long-term computer use.

CHAPTER 6

Commercial and marketing roles

One of the most significant developments resulting from increased confidence in the internet is the opportunity for individuals as well as large organisations to buy and sell products and services online. The global marketplace for sourcing goods and trading over the internet has evolved into a whole new dimension by creating new job roles and opportunities for self-employment (see also Chapter 7). This is also evident in the range of new e-business and e-marketing courses now available in higher education. In this chapter we will look at the role of an online marketing manager in some detail, including negative and positive aspects, salaries and prospects as well as skills and qualities that suit this type of work. We will also examine a number of related careers.

ONLINE MARKETING MANAGER/CONSULTANT

Online or e-marketing can provide a global shop window on an organisation's products and services and is regarded as *the* business tool of this century. This is because using the internet is proving a far more successful method of targeting customers than traditional forms of marketing. As an online marketing manager, your role will be to utilise the best and most effective marketing strategies to meet the business and commercial needs of your company. This could be negotiating affiliate marketing with other organisations or email marketing within current customer contacts or networks. You will also need to keep abreast of trends in viral marketing that uses techniques in existing social networks to produce increases in brand awareness, as well as developments in direct marketing in B2C (business-to-customer) and/or B2B environments. This might include harnessing the potential of services like Google Ads. With e-marketing particularly you will need to keep up with spam legislation as what may be a good idea to reach your potential customers could have far-reaching consequences for your business if you step outside the law. However, not all roles will be at the seemingly glitzy commercial end of promoting products and increasing sales. You might work for a small organisation, possibly in public service, where your role is to keep a network of colleagues up to date and informed on important news items, policy changes and helpful resources to support their professional development.

POSITIVE AND NEGATIVE ASPECTS

As a successful online marketing manager you will be playing a crucial role in your organisation's ability to attract new customers and increase sales. Using web-based publicity – unlike most newspaper and magazine promotions – can also have a long-term benefit as work you might have produced months or even years ago could still be picked up by search engines. Marketing is essentially a creative process using a wide variety of skills and intuition. One task you might have is to increase significant traffic to your website and you can get a real buzz when statistical analysis confirms your e-marketing strategies have been pivotal to your site's renewed popularity. These successes, however, bring with them their very own challenges and pitfalls. Most small businesses do not have the resources or expertise to compete with the powerful media rich e-marketing organisations. Also, there may be considerable pressure in an increasingly competitive marketplace to deliver improvements. Added to that are other considerations, such as the risk of getting your domain black-listed for sending large volumes of emails.

PROSPECTS

Providing you have proven e-marketing experience and ability there is excellent potential to increase responsibility and skills within a large company or with different organisations. As you become more experienced, there may be opportunities for self-employment and offering consultancy services, particularly to smaller companies who may have very limited e-marketing budgets.

AVERAGE SALARIES

Salaries for online marketing managers can range between £20 000 and £65 000 a year depending on experience and the type of organisation you work for. Consultants could earn more depending on how much business they retain year on year.

SIMILAR OR SHARED JOB ROLES AND SKILLS, BUT ARE THERE ANY DIFFERENCES?

As seen from the at-a-glance comparison chart (page 19), online marketing consultants can share similar or the same commercial and marketing skills with other related job roles. In some cases they might perform exactly the same requirements as a job advertised under a different name! To help with this confusion we have included below the job roles which are most closely related in functional skills, but also briefly commented where possible variances occur. Do also check out the recommended job-hunting agencies mentioned in Chapter 9. It is by comparing these specific job functions with your own skills that you can identify your interest or suitability for a given job role.

E-COMMERCE MANAGER/ HEAD OF E-COMMERCE

As an e-commerce manager you may be responsible for all aspects of the web work in your organisation including developing the web strategy, managing the web team and driving the web budget. There is some overlap with web developers (see page 20), but you are likely to have most control over the commercial operations of promoting and selling product and related customer services. Depending on the size of organisation, you could also be involved with buying and merchandising as well as distribution.

ONLINE SALES/ACCOUNT MANAGER

As an online sales manager your role is likely to be of an account-type nature where you might be assigned to a specific account list of agencies or client organisations. Primarily, you will work proactively with them to create new and improved sales opportunities. The role can be quite pressurised as you may have to hit target revenue goals in defined accounts. Crucially you will maintain expert knowledge of the current online marketing landscape and future trends and be able to convey such expertise to clients. It is likely that your role will also include working closely with customers to analyse and optimise creative/media campaigns and implement strategies which drive client satisfaction, revenue growth and client retention.

E-COMMERCE ANALYST

Your role as an e-commerce analyst will vary depending on the type of organisation you work for, but you are likely to be responsible for any web-based releases and have web content tools to assess the feasibility and impact of new online services. Central to the quality assurance process you will review the quality of the web system's requirements, oversee developments and implementations and then guarantee reliability and continuity 24/7. You will also proactively track issues and concerns that require effective resolution.

SKILLS AND ABILITIES

ONLINE MARKETING MANAGER/CONSULTANT

Many of the natural skills and abilities that might attract you to traditional marketing will also apply to e-marketing, but do look out below for those likely to relate specifically to promoting goods and services online:

- enjoyment of using computers and particularly web-based media

- knowledge and interest in traditional marketing and online press and trade journals

- passion for communicating and selling creative ideas

- ability to take up the challenge of leading and motivating a team

- excellent organisational and planning skills

- extensive knowledge of conducting business online

- keen sense of recognising new sales opportunities

- up-to-date and broad knowledge of internet technologies and developments

- excellent spoken and written communication skills

- ability to work under pressure and to deadlines

- business sense and awareness of importance of keeping to budget

- knowledge of a wide range of marketing techniques

- ability to react quickly to changing circumstances

- total self-motivation in establishing and maintaining client business.

RELATED OR ADDITIONAL SKILL NEEDS

E-COMMERCE ANALYST
As an e-commerce analyst you will have considerable knowledge of site optimisation techniques and developments, but in addition, and depending on the type of organisation you work for, you are likely to require additional abilities and skills in the following areas:

- risk, change and release management for a web-based environment

- finance and accountancy management

- predicting future e-commerce trends

- service delivery and implementation

- keeping up to date with specialist financial and commercial trade press and journals

- efficient release management strategies involving relevant stakeholders and stability.

ONLINE SALES/ACCOUNT MANAGER

Some organisations are exclusively e-commerce marketing outlets for specialist or wide-ranging products. Others might have retail outlets as well. In either case, you are likely to also need:

- excellent customer relation and negotiation skills

- ability to work within financial constraints and to budget.

Online/E-Marketing Executive
Sample of employer requirements

With a good understanding of the operation of the internet, search engine optimisation and online marketing techniques, you will be employed to optimise the online presence of the business. Essential requirements include: marcomms (marketing and communications) experience, good PC and Photoshop skills and attention to detail. Also good English ability and an eye for online design and presentation.

Case Study 3
Toby Grimshaw – C-Film online media manager, Careersbox

C-Film is a specialist film activation, visibility and viewing service enabling films to be activated in any website without draining an organisation's resources.

How did you get your first job - and what was it?

Using my language, IT and keyboard skills, gained through my degree, I actually started as a temp providing support to a sales and marketing department for a large insurance company based in London (1988). The role evolved as I helped streamline and improve the mode of communication for their teams. The tools were very different at the time - i.e. no internet, no mobile phones etc - compared to life today but the principle was the same: right message, right time to the right people. It was at this point that I realised that communication and understanding the different types of media available was the key driver for my career.

During the last 20 years, I have been involved in multiple sectors and business environments focusing on communications within the sales and marketing environments leading me to my current role.

What has helped you to progress?

The overriding factor in helping me progress has been an insatiable desire to ask questions of those I am dealing with, be that fellow work colleagues, clients or potential clients. This, combined with a love of being abreast of the latest media available to communicate and, in particular, the use of online film delivery tools, has helped me stay one step ahead in the media marketplace.

Do you think your educational background was helpful preparation and if so how?

Studying two foreign languages with overseas placements while at college gave me the experience of communicating in challenging circumstances. The key skills of communication and understanding the differing media mechanisms were more valuable than the actual content of my chosen subjects. Despite all the new ways to communicate I have found that one key motor skill, which I had to learn at college, was to be able to touch-type - the time investment has paid out many times over as I am able to complete proposals, documents, emails etc at a far faster rate.

Can you summarise a typical working day?
My current role focuses on the management of the film media we have created and determining how to maximise the exposure of the films through our unique C-mail (film to user's emailing service). A typical project day will be:

- update latest film content to the *free* national careers film library www.careersbox.co.uk. This shows real people doing real jobs, in film rather than written format.

- plan and deliver C-mail campaigns of specific film content to specific audiences, for example over 7000 careers professionals, internal client communications (e.g. BT) and the latest updates to Institute of Career Guidance (ICG) members. We deliver films to the inbox of any profiled audience using C-mail.

- assess and report on new film club members.

- assess and report on film and C-mail film viewing metrics – everything we do is measurable in terms of viewing, referrals etc and all are reported back to the client.

- work with our production teams on new film content to be managed into the online environments, e.g. we are currently working on a project for the Institute of Motor Industry (IMI) producing and C-mailing over 90 film case study job profiles for the motor trade.

- help organisations, such as employers, training providers etc, better understand the power of film media used in an effective manner online in a much more cost-effective and measurable way.

What are the best things and worst things about your job?
The best aspect of my role is developing new and unique e-tools using film as the central medium which then help people make better more informed choices. The C-mail service did not exist 12 months ago and is now changing how

employers and careers professionals attract and engage with their target audiences.

When individuals comment on the quality of both the films and the free services we provide, I go home happy.

The only downside of my job is the frustration that on occasions other organisations are unable to work as quickly as we do in implementing projects.

Have you any advice for school leavers wishing to enter a career in online media?
I can only share my own experiences here:

- I work in the film media marketplace using the latest technologies, which is a very competitive but fascinating and ever-changing industry. This arena is very broad and I would advise someone to focus on an area they love. For me it is the skills arena helping individuals access better media to make better more informed choices.

- as a potential employer I now look at candidates not in just their key skill-set but also in their ability to communicate effectively and their passion for what they do. Individuals can be trained and moulded but only if the desire is there.

- ensure you love the environment you're in. Keep abreast of latest changes through continually reading, seeing and experiencing the online environments you wish to work in.

Can you identify any qualities that are likely to help someone succeed?
This is a hard question to answer as we are all individuals. However, I have found it important to always take time out to consider where you are at – this is applicable to both actual workloads but also for your career path. Yes, you need drive,

determination and passion, but also ensure you review and reassess where your career is heading and, if needed, do make the change.

What do you think the future holds for you?
We are working at the forefront of both the online film media and skills marketplace and so the future will be fast moving but very exciting. The use of online film tools, such as www.careersbox.co.uk, the film club and C-mail will continue to grow. We are now working on some pioneering projects to enhance further the use of film media for e-learning and training so it's a great time for the right individuals to become involved in the sector.

And finally ...
The only final point I would like to convey is that your career is a journey which never ends. I am learning new skills every day and adding to my experience pool. Just keep asking the questions and keep on learning.

Reality Check!
We have now uncovered a number of job roles and the skills and abilities you will need to make a successful career in the internet. Before exploring home-working and self-employment and the all-important training and qualifications you might require for a career in the internet, we hope you are beginning to sense a real interest, even passion, in one or a number of the following areas:

● **how the internet works** – this is the scientific and/or technical end of web-based careers. In some cases, you may never meet a client. In others, for example as a web developer, you could be involved with a customer and a large team of colleagues from first meeting to site completion and going live.

- **how it looks** – this involves all aspects of the highly innovative and creative process where you are responsible for visualising and designing appropriate images and incorporating multimedia audio, film, newsfeeds and links.

- **how it feels** – you are constantly concerned with the quality and use of website editorial and content, its impact on web users and its compatibility to your organisation's key objectives.

- **how it sells** – this involves the commercial and marketing aspects of the internet and offers an intoxicating mixture of innovation, creativity and business enterprise.

CHAPTER 7

Home-working and self-employment

Our ancestors, just a few generations ago, could never have imagined how commonplace it would be for individuals to work and earn a living while still being at home. Improved computer technology, software and faster broadband speeds have all contributed to the exponential growth in both the number as well as the range of job possibilities now available. While the number of self-made entrepreneurs buying and selling niche products and services online has grown with the technology, there has also been a significant trend towards more flexible home-working arrangements. For example, business employees have secure access to their organisation's extranet services, which make it possible to locate documents and files previously only available by going to the office. It is now possible to work from home for just a few hours, or perhaps one or two days a week, or in more exceptional cases all but full-time.

There are also significant advantages to working from home particularly for parents with small children, as an increase in home-working roles can provide an invaluable opportunity to maintain skills while balancing important home and family commitments. There are encouragingly also greater opportunities than ever for people with disabilities to compete effectively in the job market with new internet job agencies brokering work for individuals online. It is the convenience and particularly cost-savings of working from home that has particularly influenced business entrepreneurs and created an amazing range of job opportunities. New business start-ups are successfully trading longer than ever before with resources available on the internet as well as excellent support from national, regional and local business advice and networking organisations. It is also easier than ever to complete VAT returns, conduct banking transactions and order stock online, thereby reducing staffing overheads and time spent on administration.

EMPLOYMENT TRENDS

According to some international surveys, self-employment has increased substantially in Western countries. In Canada, for example, since the 1990s, it has significantly outpaced paid employment growth by an average year-to-year rate of 3.3 per cent versus 0.2 per cent. Self-employment is also highest for those aged 50-plus, supporting the theory that it may be used as a transition out of the labour force, with as many as one in four men aged 50–65 being self-employed in 2006. Whatever the reasons, it is likely that technology of the future will play an increasing role in supporting home-working and new self-employment opportunities. According to National Statistics (Labour Market Trends Oct 2005) in the UK home-workers – defined as people who work mainly in their own home, or in different places using home as a base – is known to be 3.1 million out of 28.76 million, or 11 per cent of the total workforce. It is likely – with improved broadband speeds, increasing concern about the environmental impact of travel and associated costs – that this figure is set to increase substantially in the future.

SELF-EMPLOYMENT AND THE INTERNET

Much will depend on your personal circumstances, abilities, skills and experience, but be encouraged as the internet and use of email for promotion and networking is liberating self-employment and home-working opportunities. As you will see from Graham Wood's case study summary below, it seems that there is much we can learn from his experience after five years in self-employment, beginning with some of the benefits of using the internet in his business and following on with his excellent advice for anyone wishing to start up in this popular area. Later we will explore a number of home-working examples that rely totally on the internet for an income.

Case Study 4
Graham Wood – Hazelwood Sound and Vision

Hazelwood Sound and Vision specialises in providing audiovisual and sound reinforcement solutions that improve communications in public buildings.

What are the main benefits and uses of the internet to your business?

- Online banking – BACS (bankers automated clearing service) payments, statements enabling money management/cash flow. However, security of internet bank accounts is a very real threat, so consider enlisting a good IT person early on.

- Emails – quicker and cheaper correspondence than letters by post, invoicing, and receipt of regular e-zines.

- Web – research products, makes, models, specifications, sourcing solutions to problems and where to source products from.

- Transfer of large files across the world (yousendit.com) near instantly.

- Remote access to office-based data (through VPN).

- VoIP for very low-cost telephone calls.

What is a typical working day?
Office based: admin – accounts, emails, post, filing, office tidying, sales proposals, IT issues, business network breakfasts, training courses (attending), exhibitions (attending), marketing (not enough) – 10–12 days per month.

Client based: usually for installations but also sales calls, and after-sales/service calls – 8–10 days per month.

What are the best and worst aspects of working from home?
Best – flexibility to schedule my day as I wish; no travelling to my office; can fit in family things as part of my day (e.g. shopping in the day on my way back home); can pay myself bonus for my birthday/Christmas; mobile phone calls covered as a business expense.

Worst – can be long hours in order to handle peaks of work; can't take long holidays yet (no staff cover!); delegation (to whom?); too much time working *in* the business and not enough *on* the business; not getting enough sleep; not switching off at 6p.m.; difficult to increase margins unless have a unique product or service. Your partner may need to support you financially in the early years in order to meet household bills. Consider *not* employing your partner in the business so as to reduce the risk to family life if/when the business goes through a bad patch. Too much time spent ineffectively – if I reduced my admin time by 50 per cent I would have a four-day working week for the same income!

What advice would you have for anyone wishing to start up in audiovisual installations or productions?

- Get experience in a wide range of activities by working for other companies as a freelancer first.

- Production work is about teamwork, so learn what your strengths and weaknesses are.

- Understand that cash flow is *critical* to the running of *any* business.

- Market research *before* setting up – get some professional advice on how to if necessary, *then* invest in the business (not the other way around).

- Build a business budget that pays a (small) monthly income *every* month by setting up a bank standing order. As the business grows, so can the income you pay into your personal or joint (non-business) bank account. This provides a monthly target to aim for and helps with household budgeting.

What does the future hold for the audiovisual industry as new technologies evolve?

- 20 years ago the PC was just becoming something that could do something useful – spreadsheets and word-processors etc.

- Now the IP (internet protocol) is everywhere and taking over – pretty much every piece of equipment is a stand-alone computer in disguise! Tomorrow's employees will need to understand how to configure and use IP-based systems as much as audio and video systems.

- Hardware will continue to fall in price so the margins from selling 'boxes' will progressively reduce.

- Competition from internet suppliers buying in bulk with low storage costs means a *constant* search for new products and solutions before they become commodities.

HOME-WORKING AND THE INTERNET

Self-employment and home-working can be one and the same. For example, a web designer or web developer (covered in greater detail in other chapters) can be self-employed or work as a consultant almost totally from home. However, it is important also to highlight a number of other internet job roles which are increasingly made possible through online agencies offering online work. This relatively new phenomena is set to increase as employers place ever-greater demands on fewer staff to the point where individuals choose to opt out, even earn less, rather than be constantly pressurised at work. For others, the freedom to work from home and accept or decline work can be very appealing. Also, as previously mentioned, the internet offers greater opportunities and more flexible work patterns for individuals with disabilities. In recent years, there has been a huge improvement in accessibility for both visually and hearing-impaired people from the Web Accessibility Initiative (WAI), which develops strategies, guidelines, and resources to help make the web more open to these groups. The hope is that employment opportunities will increase.

Sample of Online Agencies Offering Online Work

Customer service	Secretarial services
Internet and telephone sales	Teleworking
Marketing and design services	Translation services
Proofreading	Virtual assistants
Research bureau	Virtual Office Services
Web design	

CHAPTER 8

Training and qualifications

We hope by now that you have uncovered some helpful insights and information to confirm your interest and suitability or otherwise to a career in the internet. It is from exploring the different job roles, skills and personal qualities that you can make a more informed decision as to whether you want to pursue a career in the internet. This chapter is designed to take your research a stage further by landscaping the many different routes you might take, whether you are starting out for the first time, currently studying or perhaps thinking about changing your career.

To help you decide the most appropriate route for you, we have provided information around a series of typical scenarios, and tailored appropriate academic or vocational choices that you might be facing. Do take time to consider all the options open to you, using the scenarios to anticipate potential means of achieving your goals. It is not possible to be too prepared: don't let life happen to you, but realise your ambitions are possible with careful planning and research. Your enjoyment and ultimate success will depend to some extent on accurately assessing the way by which you learn best and matching this to the level to which you want to pursue your education. Most of all, your enjoyment and success will be ensured or denied by your level of motivation and dedication.

FASCINATING FACTS

While very specific experience, training and qualifications will be required for most technical and scientific, design and audiovisual careers involving the internet, content and information as well as commercial and marketing roles will depend very much on your educational and employment experience.

SCENARIO A

'I'm thinking about employment, but also possibly staying on in further education.'

We do recommend such important decisions are discussed fully with your family, teachers and your local careers/Connexions adviser. Should you be seeking work it will be important to check out the local employment opportunities with particular regard to the training available to you; establish whether companies are offering IT Apprenticeship or other recognised day-release qualifications, or in-company training schemes. How long it will take to reach Levels 4 and 5 in particular, will vary widely depending on the size and type of organisation you work for. As you can see below, a number of alternative academic and vocational routes offer you excellent opportunities to suit your particular circumstances.

The diplomas referred to in the following section are a new vocational qualification for 14–19-year-olds being introduced gradually throughout England from September 2008–2013. There is a specialist IT Diploma available at Levels 1 (Foundation), 2 (Higher) and 3 (Advanced), which will be regarded as equal in stature to existing qualifications such as GCSEs and A/AS levels, the difference between them lying in the learning method and structure. All diploma courses are being developed in partnership with employers and so combine classroom learning with practical hands-on experience. The diploma will also provide a sound alternative route into higher education. For further and regularly updated information, including where courses can be studied, visit http://yp.direct.gov.uk/diplomas.

Acronyms used in the next section and not encountered before are as follows: AVCE (A level Vocational Certificate of Education); BTEC (Business and Technical Education Council); GCSE (General Certificate of Secondary Education); GNVQ (General National Vocational Qualification); ICT (Information and Communications Technology); ITQ (Information Technology Qualification); NVQ (National Vocational Qualification); OCR (Oxford and Cambridge RSA Examinations); SQA (Scottish Qualifications Authority); SVQ (Scottish Vocational Qualification); and SWAP (Scottish Wider Access Programme).

1. LEAVING SCHOOL WITH LEVEL 1 FOUNDATION QUALIFICATIONS

GCSEs; BTEC Introductory; Foundation Diploma; NVQ/SVQ Level 1; or City & Guilds Level 1 Certificates.

You still automatically qualify for entry to Level 2 courses at your local college. This can include retake or new GCSEs. However, if you can secure suitable employment with a suitable company you may continue to Level 2 intermediate vocational courses with examples such as:

- BTEC/SQA First Certificate/Diploma in computing, IT practitioners

- Higher Diploma in IT

- NVQ/SVQ IT

- City & Guilds ICT systems.

Some organisations may offer you an Apprenticeship or Modern Apprenticeship (Scotland) resulting in NVQ/SVQ qualifications in Information Technology.

2. LEAVING SCHOOL OR COLLEGE WITH LEVEL 2 INTERMEDIATE QUALIFICATIONS

GCSEs/S grades (A*–C/1–3); BTEC/SQA First Certificate or First Diploma; OCR Level 2; Higher Diploma; NVQ/SVQ Level 2; or City & Guilds Level 2.

It may well be in your interests to apply for Level 3 courses, at the same or a different local college, while you could also look for a suitable employer offering examples such as:

- BTEC/SQA National/Certificates for IT practitioners

- OCR ICT

- Advanced Diploma in IT

- NVQ/SVQ in ICT

- City & Guilds Advanced Diploma in ICT systems

- BTEC/Higher National Diploma in e-business

- OCR Certificate/Diploma for i-media users

- NVQ/SVQ ITQ for IT Users.

Some employers may offer different specialist IT/web-based courses depending on their business needs. However, you could also consider following an Advanced/Higher Apprenticeship or Modern Apprenticeship (Scotland) resulting in NVQ/SVQ qualifications in IT. See further information and web links in Chapter 9.

FASCINATING FACT

E-skills UK merges IT and Telecoms professionals' apprenticeship frameworks. The telecommunications, computing and networking fields are converging, and moving from hardware intensive to software intensive platforms. Embedded voice communications capability is already part of emerging offerings on the internet. Increasingly, the management of voice, data, video and location information will converge in information-based services (e-skills UK 2008).

3. LEAVING SCHOOL OR COLLEGE WITH LEVEL 3 ADVANCED QUALIFICATIONS

AS and A2 levels/H Grades; BTEC/SQA National; OCR Level 3; Advanced Diploma; NVQ/SVQ; City & Guilds Level 3; Access to HE.

Much will depend on the subjects you studied and your results, but you may qualify for entry into Level 4 professional/management, or higher education (university) qualifications in web development, web design or multimedia courses. Applying to university doesn't give you an obligation to go, so it might be wise to apply, even if you plan on finding suitable IT or web-based employment. If successful in finding employment you could train whilst working, taking further internal or external courses. Some employers will encourage staff to pursue foundation degrees whereby you are paid a salary while learning (see Scenario C).

Web Developer
Qualification and training profile

We have already discovered that web developers are at the forefront of scientific and technical innovation and it is therefore not surprising to discover that most employers expect applicants to have at least a degree-level education (see scenarios D–F). However, the British Computer Society offers respected professional awards in IT and computing at certificate, diploma and professional graduate diploma level. Indeed, a further route in is the undergraduate, postgraduate or work-based training programmes undertaken through the e-skills Graduate Professional Development Award (GPDA), also well regarded. As is the Certified Internet Web Professional (CIW) web development course, entertained by many employers and available independently, which confirms skills across a range of software and systems. See Case Study 5 on page 86. If you are a career changer do examine Scenario G for possible alternative routes depending on related or non-related experience.

Colleges and universities provide a wide range of computer-based and multimedia-related courses which will equip you

---

with the essential training and qualifications needed. For example, employers will be looking out for experience in a number of the following programming/scripting languages: Java, HTML, XML, XHTML, Perl, ASP, PHP, Javascript, ActionScript, CGI, CSS, SSL, SQL and MySQL databases and security technologies. You should also be familiar with one or more of the common web development packages, including; HotMetal Pro, Axure RP, Creative Suite (includes Dreamweaver, Flash and Fireworks), Coldfusion, Adobe GoLive, and Visual Interdev. For most of the technical names listed above, see jargon busters on page 92.

Web Designer
Qualification and training profile

Despite the fact that formal qualifications are not required for this career, most designers will have had experience either from other design disciplines, such as graphics or multimedia, or have taken training in web design software. This can be by self-study, such as the CIW master designer course, at university (see page 86), the Open University, or on an established part- or full-time college course. For example, college courses can provide a good grounding in technical and design basics with specialist Levels 1–3 courses such as:

- BTEC interactive use of media

- OCR Certificate for IT users

- CLAiT Plus and CLAiT Advanced

- OCR i-media

- City & Guilds IT users awards (Diploma and Advanced Diploma).

These courses will also introduce you to one or a number of design packages such as Photoshop, Dreamweaver, Flash, Fireworks and GoLive. Also, so that you have flexibility and control over your designs, courses will help you understand coding, scripting and programming languages such as: Active Server Pages (ASP), JavaScript, CSS, HTML, DHTML and XML, and PHP.

For most of the technical names listed above, see jargon busters on page 92.

SCENARIO B

'I'm in work, but want to improve my skills and job prospects.'

Foundation degrees (England, Northern Ireland and Wales) are an alternative to undergraduate degrees and HNDs (Higher National Diploma), but are still degree-level qualifications with many students studying whilst they are employed in order to improve their prospects. They will equip you with the knowledge, understanding and skills relevant to your employment and are usually delivered by colleges and universities (and sometimes by other training providers). A full-time course will usually take you two years to complete, a part-time course may take longer and you will not necessarily need traditional academic qualifications to gain entry to a course. Many courses have flexible teaching arrangements involving part-time or evening attendance at college, distance learning or learning via the internet. After completing their foundation degree some students go on to study for an honours degree (which usually takes one further year).

Course titles will vary but listed in Figure 2 are samples of IT and internet courses currently offered.

FIGURE 2: IT AND INTERNET COURSE TITLES

Creative digital communications	E-technology	Digital technologies
Design and development of e-learning	Applied digital media	Technology
Creative technologies and enterprise	Creative multimedia	Multimedia
Design for interactive new media	Digital media design	Network management
Moving image and web-based media	Multimedia (design/ games art)	

SCENARIO C

'I left education with few qualifications, but am now really keen on higher education.

Access to HE courses (England, Wales and Northern Ireland) and SWAP (Scotland) provide a route into higher education if you do not have the qualifications which are usually required. They will prepare you with the knowledge and skills needed for university-level study and lead to an award of the Access to HE qualification/SWAP, equivalent to Level 3.

Study patterns differ between courses, but usually include a combination of specific subjects relevant to the progression route as well as more general skills, usually including English, mathematics and IT. Courses are commonly available as full-time, one-year, or part-time courses which can be studied over two or more years, sometimes including evening study. Most courses are delivered in further education colleges, although some adult education centres, community centres and universities offer Access to HE courses.

Some Access to HE courses provide preparation for particular HE programmes such as teaching, nursing, humanities, sciences and social sciences. Many courses are titled Access to HE allowing entry to a wide range of degree and HND courses, while others may be particularly relevant to IT and the internet including the examples in Figure 3.

FIGURE 3: IT AND INTERNET ACCESS COURSE TITLES

Digital/creative media	Engineering and technology	Computer science
Business and ICT	Information Technology	Multimedia
IT, computing and business	Mathematics, IT and statistics	Art and design
Art foundation and creative computing	Visual communication	

OPEN UNIVERSITY – POSSIBLE OPTION FROM ALL SCENARIOS!

Do also consider the ultimately flexible Open University study route, which offers many excellent opportunities ranging from Level 1 short study courses through to diploma, certificate, undergraduate and postgraduate qualifications. The OU is a distance learning university whose 'supported open learning' methods are designed to help you with self-study. Students pursue learning at a time that suits them, within a framework of overall deadlines to aid organisation, benefiting from having a tutor on hand for support.

Case Study 5
Chris Wallace – Open University Web Design Course

Chris Wallace represents an increasing number of students seeking to avoid getting into debt at university, instead pursuing paid employment alongside studying through the Open University. Chris's current job is as a shift-worker in a regional Boots distribution centre.

What is the name of your course and qualification attained on completion?
CIW – this is a recognised international course in the IT industry. See www.ciwcertified.com/certifications/program.asp.

How long will it take?
There isn't a set time deadline on this course as it's all based on the time you have around your work, although I am taking my course over two to three years.

How did you hear about Open University?
I was searching the internet looking for a specific course in website design and came across the CIW and then discovered this could be completed by distance learning with the OU.

What was the main appeal/reasons for doing OU?
I chose OU because I didn't get the grades at college to get into university, but the flexible study route particularly appealed as I could also carry on with my job.

What are the technical implications of studying online?
You have a course book with all of your work in as well as two CDs. One is for the TMAs (tutor marked assignments) and the other has some of the course work on it. You send your work via email and there is help from tutors on their website and over the phone. I usually complete two assignments a week, which takes two days, and always get a response from my tutor within two to three days, which I think is excellent.

What were the early weeks/months like and what helped you to progress – keep motivated?
I found the early stages fine but that is because I already had some knowledge of website programming. You have to be motivated to do an OU course, because you have to direct your own study. The OU is very flexible though, so you can fit it around full-time work.

Do you think your educational background was helpful preparation and if so how?
I have two IT qualifications from school and college. One is a GNVQ and the other is an AVCE. There was a unit in each of these courses on website programming which served as a useful introduction. I think that I would have found this course extremely hard if I didn't have some knowledge.

Can you summarise a typical study week/day?
As this course is all done via the internet, you can get about two bits of coursework done a week. You have to send them off via email to be marked, then you have to wait for them to be sent back to you. I find that you can get a piece of coursework done in one day.

What are the best things and worst things about OU study?
The best thing is that you do not have the pressure of doing your work in class with lots of people around you. I always found that distracting. At the same time, that can be the worst thing because you have to keep yourself motivated at home to finish the course!

Have you any advice for school leavers wishing to enter a career as a website designer?
Yes, if you are going the OU route you have to be very self-motivated and work hard at keeping to a study routine. OU courses are a great way to impress potential employers as they can identify straight away that you are prepared to work hard and if necessary quite independently. Also, as the course is specifically aimed at, in my case design, they know I'm totally committed in career terms.

Can you identify any qualities that are likely to help someone succeed?
You need patience as programming can take a long time; especially when there are 50-plus lines of code and you need to look for the error that's causing a fault. Also, it helps if you can work in a team, as it's very unlikely you will be the only one on a project.

What do you think the future holds for you and the industry?
As the internet is still growing at a rapid rate, there is always going to be a demand for website designers – almost every organisation, business or charity needs one! However, I'm keen to be self-employed as, again, that offers the freedom I like and have made a start with my own site at www.grafixrevolution.co.uk.

FASCINATING FACT

The Open University is Britain's largest university with 200 000 students. See www.open.ac.uk.

SCENARIO D
'I definitely want to go university.'

This is ideal preparation for a career in the internet, as a degree potentially opens a number of doors. There is unprecedented opportunity to specialise, with a choice of over 1000 different courses on offer. These can be from two-year HNDs (which provide an option to migrate to a third year of a degree on successful completion), to three, four or five-year Bachelor of Arts (BA), Master of Arts (MA, Scotland), or Bachelor of Science (BSc) degrees, which can contain industrial placements if termed a 'sandwich course'.

You may wish to explore single, joint or combined honours degrees, but for detailed course descriptions and specific entry requirements do refer to individual colleges and universities.

As indicated in Scenario A, you will need to be leaving school or college with Level 3 advanced qualifications. These can be AS and A2 levels/H Grades; BTEC/SQA National; OCR Level 3; Advanced Diploma (new from 2008); NVQ/SVQ, City & Guilds Level 3; or Access to HE qualifications. In the meantime, listed in Figures 4, 5, 6 and 7 are just examples of the vast range of web and internet-based courses listed on the UCAS website, with particular reference to this publication's emphasis on: scientific and technical, design and audiovisual, content and information, and commercial and marketing courses.

FIGURE 4: TECHNICAL AND SCIENTIFIC UNIVERSITY COURSES

Applied information technology internet

Creative technologies

New media production technology

Multi media systems development

Integrated technology

Computing and internet technology

Software product design (internet app)

Mobile computing

Web technologies

Internet engineering and web management

Internet computing

Computer software engineering

Information security and forensic computing

Communication systems

Mobile media technology

Web development

Web technology

Multimedia and website development

Computer science

Web development and management

Mobile and interactive TV development

Internet technology

Web applications development

Ethical hacking and counter measures

Internet engineering

Computer science (games)

FIGURE 5: DESIGN AND AUDIOVISUAL UNIVERSITY COURSES

Multimedia web production

Video game design

Creative online design

Computing interactive design

Creative technologies

Interactive multimedia design

Internet management and web design

Graphic and web design

Multimedia communication systems

New media design

Computer gaming design

Web design and multimedia

Digital media design

Digital interactive media

Creative digital media

Audio and internet
technology
Moving image and web-
based media
Animation

Design management and
innovation
Design for digital media

Computer games technology

FIGURE 6: CONTENT AND INFORMATION UNIVERSITY COURSES

Information systems
and management
English with multimedia
technologies
Internet information
systems
Information communications
technology
Web, multimedia and
business information
Multimedia learning
technologies
Information and IT
Journalism studies with
internet technology
Computer science with
knowledge and information
systems

Information technology with
English language
Multimedia journalism

Information and library
studies
Creative and professional
writing
Media communication (web
and new media)
Web and multimedia
journalism
Administration and IT
Creative studies

FIGURE 7: COMMERCIAL AND MARKETING UNIVERSITY COURSES

Mobile media technology

Web enterprise

E-business technology
and management

E-commerce and
internet systems

E-business

Business and
e-business strategies

Internet management
and web design

Computer science with marketing

E-commerce and digital
business

Computing for business and
e-commerce

M-commerce

E-commerce computing
(marketing)

Internet technology and
e-commerce

New media innovation

E-commerce systems

Jargon Busters

.NET product by Microsoft – it is essentially a
language-neutral platform for enterprise and web
development. The aim is to provide an abstract machine
for professional developers, covering both traditional IT
client/server and n-tier programs and web-oriented
applications.

Adobe company that builds award-winning software
solutions for network publishing, including web, print, video,
wireless and broadband applications. Its graphic design,
imaging, dynamic media and authoring tools enable people to
create, publish and deliver visually rich content for various
types of media.

Ajax asynchronous JavaScript and XML – a programming
technique for creating interactive web applications. Small
amounts of data are exchanged as needed instead of pulling

entire webpages to be reloaded each time the user makes a change. This increases the webpage's response time, interactivity and overall usability.

API application program interface – interface between the operating system and the application programs, it extends the capabilities of web servers. Used by programmers who write applications that can interact with other applications, a server API is a published interface.

ASP application service provider – a specialised form of internet service provider that allows a company to have a software application hosted for a rental fee. An ASP sells access to a suite of applications which is typically licensed from an applications vendor.

Active Server Pages specification developed by Microsoft for a dynamically created webpage that utilises ActiveX scripting, usually VB script or Jscript code. When a web browser requests an ASP page, the web server generates a page with HTML code and sends it back to the browser.

C# pronounced C-sharp – a programming language used in Microsoft's .NET product, it technically looks a lot like Java (and Microsoft's Java offering, Visual J++).

CGI common gateway interface – a standard script for running programs on a server from a webpage. CGI programs (also called scripts) can be run independently and were designed to be external so they can run under various (possibly different) servers interchangeably.

Coldfusion a rapid application development (RAD) system created by Allaire Corporation (which merged with Macromedia), it integrates browser, server and database technologies into web applications.

CSS cascading style sheets – format used to separate style from structure on webpages, it is a feature of HTML that gives both web developers and users more control over how webpages are displayed.

DHTML   dynamic HTML – dubbed a next-generation HTML, this is a mark-up language that describes how text and images are displayed on a webpage.

Flash   short for Macromedia Flash – a vector graphic animation technology that's bandwidth friendly and browser-independent. In other words, it is a programming technique that enables movies and animation to move seamlessly across a web browser.

HTML   hypertext mark-up language – mark-up language (versus a programming language) that uses tags to structure text into headings, paragraphs, lists and links and tells a web browser how to display text and images.

J2EE   Java 2 Enterprise Edition – important technology in some large companies, it uses distributed computing to answer queries. Developed by Sun Microsystems, J2EE is considered an app server.

languages   if computers communicate with each other in protocols, then people communicate with computers through programming languages. Like human languages, there are many dialects and versions designed to run on specific machines or operating systems. The most widely used web programming languages are: Ada, Basic, C++, Fortran, Java, Lisp, Perl, PostScript, Prolog, Snobol, and Visual Basic.

marcomms   marketing and communications

Perl   practical extraction and report language – script programming language used to process text. It runs on many platforms (including Windows and Macintosh) and is installed on most Unix workstations. It is available free and allows web developers to write code quickly or perform system administration tasks.

PHP   personal home page

SQL   structured query language *(pronounced: see-quill)* – standardised query language used for requesting information from a database. The original version (called SEQUEL, for Structured English Query Language) was designed at an IBM research centre in 1974 and 1975. SQL was introduced as a commercial database system by Oracle in 1979, and it refers to either of two database management software products from Sybase and Microsoft.

SQL server   relational database management system (RDBMS) – the SQL server was designed for client/server use and is accessed by applications using SQL. It runs on OS/2, Windows NT, NetWare servers, VAXen, and Unix workstations. Generically, it is any database management system (DBMS) that can respond to queries from client machines formatted in the SQL language.

VLE   virtual learning environment – a standardised, computer-based environment that supports the delivery of web-based learning and facilities online.

XML   eXtensible mark-up language – programming language/specification developed by the W3C. XML is a pared-down version of SGML, designed especially for web documents. It enables web authors and web developers to create their own customised tags to provide functionality not available with HTML.

Most of the above jargon busters have been reproduced by permission of © 1994–2008 NetLingo™ The Internet Dictionary at http://www.netlingo.co.

SCENARIO E

'I am a graduate thinking about continuing my studies.'

If you are a graduate of any of the degree courses mentioned above, there are many reasons why you might consider studying for a second degree, or postgraduate diploma/certificate, including:

● pursuing your chosen career, one that requires further professional qualifications

● opportunity to convert, and prepare for a new career interest

● recommended by your tutors to further develop your expertise

● improve prospects in the job market by proving thoroughgoing research efficiency.

Such choices still need to be weighed up and researched very carefully. For example, second degrees can take many different forms, and can result in the award of a master's degree, doctorate, certificate, diploma or various other professional qualifications. They will usually require applicants to have had some previous study or experience in their chosen field, typically a previous undergraduate degree. Taught postgraduate courses leading to an MA (Master of Arts) or MSc (Master of Science) degree are usually a year and similar to most undergraduate courses in that they are lecture based, with some coursework followed by an end-of-year examination.

Research degrees are usually under the supervision of an experienced researcher with Master of Philosophy (MPhil), for example, being normally one year full-time, and Doctor of Philosophy (PhD) taking a minimum of three years full-time by comparison. A doctorate involves an in-depth study of a specific subject or topic followed by a written dissertation or thesis.

Listed in Figure 8 is a small sample of full-time web-related courses you might consider.

FIGURE 8: POSTGRADUATE COURSES

Distributed and multimedia information systems

Informatics digital enterprise management

Web enterprise

Computer networks

Mobile and handheld communications

Web management

Digital media

Multimedia applications

Internet and enterprise computing

Enterprise system implementation

Information management

Digital information management

Computer science (interactive entertainment)

E-commerce

Advanced computer systems

Strategic information systems

Web design

Advanced games computing

Web services development

Advanced computing IT with multimedia

Information quality

Web design and content planning

Mobile and wireless computing

Information studies

Informatics

SCENARIO F

'I am a graduate looking for employment.'

If you are coming from a non-technical or scientific degree background then do consider the previous scenario as it could act as a useful insurance as well as filling an important skills gap. However, as an arts, humanities, social science or graduate of almost any discipline, you may be able to consider some of the content and information as well as many of the commercial and marketing jobs covered in Chapters 5 and 6. A good deal will also depend on the employed or voluntary experience you acquired whilst at university; such as involvement in clubs' or societies' website development and maintenance, writing for online or printed student magazines, faculty journals or newsletters etc. Experience of publishing, communications, public relations, marketing, media and multimedia applications would all count as experience to stand you in good stead, giving you that edge over the other candidates.

Web Content Manager
Training and qualifications profile

There are no specific qualifications or training courses to prepare for web content jobs. You could come from almost any background and, upon gaining experience within a particular organisation, move into this type of work. Any experiences though that show an aptitude for journalism, marketing, public relations and/or IT would likely give a prospective employee an edge over the other candidates in what is a highly competitive industry.

You must be able to exhibit an ability to write clearly, succinctly and with interest at interview. Ideally promoting your abilities through the exhibition of a portfolio; as it is almost certain that a candidate would have experience of writing content in some form, although not necessarily online. Examples of published materials well worth including are:

- in-house staff resources

- marketing materials, bulletins, e-newsletters

- customer brochures or educational prospectuses

- articles, leaflets and information sheets

- student magazines

- multimedia.

Specific IT skills are not required, although knowledge of web design, desktop publishing and photo-imaging would be helpful, as would an understanding of web content management systems and how they work. You are likely to be given training in specific packages once you start working.

Alternatively, you might wish to consider courses with the National Union of Journalists (NUJ) or the Society for Editors and Proofreaders (SfEP), which include training for copy-editing and proofreading (see Chapter 8).

Furthermore, if you are a graduate of computer science, mobile, multimedia, web applications, design security or a wide range of related interactive technologies, you will have trained already to a very high standard and your prospects for employment are generally very good. You may already have a BA, MA (Scotland) or BSc, but to help you consider what additional skills employers may be looking for, we have listed typical examples from a small sample of web-based job adverts (in Chapters 3, 4 and 6). These can be explored in greater depth using the sites recommended in the next chapter.

SCENARIO G

'I'm thinking of changing career ...'

This is a major decision for anyone, but if you are thinking of making a fresh start by pursuing a career in the internet it will be important to establish and encourage yourself by identifying any related or personal interest experience you have gained. For example, you may have had a career break from the IT and telecoms industry, or have innate skills or a natural acumen for all things technical. This is one sector where there are tremendous opportunities for self-development and training as well as transferable skills, as we can see from the two situations outlined below.

CAREER CHANGER – WITH RELATED EMPLOYMENT EXPERIENCE

No formal qualifications are needed to become a web developer, the medium is open to all. Having said that, with a creative and practical knowledge of what makes a site look good and easy to use, along with technical expertise of the 'back-end' systems which explain how it works, you should be off to a good start. The route to establishing yourself as a web developer will depend on previous qualifications and experience as an employer will need to be convinced of your abilities and skills. Also, if you already have proven experienced in computer programming, digital, and the multimedia industry then you are more likely to enter at a higher level, with more responsibility and be remunerated accordingly.

CAREER CHANGER – NO RELATED EMPLOYMENT EXPERIENCE

If changing career completely then your route to getting established in an internet career is likely to take longer and rely considerably on your personal interest and motivation to succeed. Here are a few suggestions that may help you get started and ultimately convince a potential employer of your suitability for this type of work.

- evidence of voluntary web-related technical or writing experience perhaps for a charity or local community organisation

- CD, DVD portfolio of projects undertaken, or a currently active website to display

- active website experience – ideally a live site you have been involved in

- pursuing part-time/evening college certificate or diploma courses

- relevant independent study or distance learning course.

Web Author/Editor
There is no set entry route, although many employers expect applicants to have a degree. Degree course subjects such as communications, journalism and multimedia may be useful. Some web authors/editors come from a background in journalism, or may have worked previously in marketing or IT.

Web authors/editors may be employed by web design companies, IT consultancies, media organisations or a company's marketing/corporate communication department. There are job opportunities throughout the UK.

The IT industry is working in a rapidly expanding global marketplace. As a result of the internet developing at great speed, there has been an explosion in the number of new roles being created, such as web author/editor. The internet is still in its infancy, with a long way to go before its fully fledged development – many internet roles are yet to exist, or are still embryonic.

Vacancies may be advertised on individual company and recruitment websites, and in trade publications, such as *Computer Weekly, Computing, Marketing and PR Week*. The local and national press also advertise positions.

Employers may look for previous experience of copywriting, supported by relevant work experience and vocational skills. Applicants may also need to have some knowledge of, or experience in, the field they are writing for. Technical computing expertise is not required, although skills in web design and desktop publishing may be useful.

CHAPTER 9

Next steps and resources

This final chapter is designed to help you delve deeper into your areas of particular interest and uncover appropriate further information. The emphasis is on providing you with web-based sources to include important careers, option choice and labour market information as well as other potentially helpful organisations. We then cross-reference our main themes with a selection of useful general sites, specific job-hunting agencies and important training and qualification sources. Finally, we have added a number of relevant publications that may also support your research towards a successful career in the internet.

CAREERS INFORMATION

JOB PROFILES - ADULTS
You will reach a general search facility with this web address (URL), but from 'Jobs and careers' can search over 400 job profiles: www10.learndirect-advice-search.co.uk.

JOBS4U - YOUNG PEOPLE
This is a highly informative resource offering A–Z, job families and articles: www.connexions-direct.com/jobs4u/.

PROSPECTS - GRADUATES

You will need to check out the jobs and work section and 'Explore types of jobs': www.prospects.ac.uk.

CAREERS SERVICE NORTHERN IRELAND

Job information is just one of the many different menu options within this excellent site: www.careersserviceni.com.

CAREERS SCOTLAND

Visit the informative and helpful 'Research a career' section for detailed careers information: www.careers-scotland.org.uk.

CAREERS WALES

The 'Careers ideas' section is a great place to explore the extensive A-Z, job groups and find-a-career support information: www.careerswales.com.

SPECIALIST CAREERS INFORMATION SITES

E-SKILLS UK

This excellent site is packed full of helpful careers information on a wide range of IT and internet-based careers. See also the video entries and information on training and qualifications. A separate entry for e-skills UK Apprenticeships is listed under 'Training and qualifications': www.e-skills.com/careers.

SKILLSET

This site includes extensive careers information for the creative industries including interactive media, computer gaming and animation: www.skillset.org.

OPTION CHOICES

The regional sites (under 'Careers information' above) include their own subject option support pages. 'Which way now' is aimed at Year 9 GCSE options: www.connexions-direct.com/whichwaynow/, and 'It's your choice' is for post-16 choices in England and Wales: www.connexions-direct.com/itsyourchoice/.

LABOUR MARKET INFORMATION (EMPLOYMENT TRENDS)

e-skills UK   www.e-skills.com/Research-and-policy/
    Insights-2008/2179
National Guidance Research Forum   www.guidance-research.org
Sector Skills Matrix   www.ssdamatrix.org.uk
National Online Management Information System   www.nomisweb.
    co.uk

GENERAL SITES

Adobe   www.adobe.com/uk/
Apple   www.apple.com/uk/
British Computer Magazines   www.wrx.zen.co.uk/mags/corner.htm
British Computer Society   www.bcs.org
British Institute of Technology & E-commerce   www.bite.ac.uk
ComputerWeekly.com Jobs   www.computerweekly.com/jobs/
Computingcareers.co.uk   www.computingcareers.co.uk
Datascope   www.datascope.co.uk
Internet Services Providers' Association   www.ispa.org.uk
Internet Watch Foundation   www.iwf.org.uk
IPTV World Forum   www.iptv-forum.com
Just IT Training and Recruitment   www.justit.co.uk
Microsoft   www.microsoft.com/en/gb/default.aspx
UK Online Centres   www.ukonlinecentres.com/consumer/
Web User   www.webuser.co.uk
What is RSS? RSS Explained   www.whatisrss.com
Wi-Fi Alliance   www.wi-fi.org
WiMax Forum   www.wimaxforum.org
Workhound   www.workhound.co.uk

TECHNICAL AND SCIENTIFIC

See also Chapter 3.
CW Jobs.co.uk   www.cwjobs.co.uk
DCSL Software   www.dcslsoftware.com
HTML Writers Guild   www.iwf.org.uk
Institution of Analysts and Programmers   www.iap.org.uk
Internet Security   www.symantec.com/specprog/ctm/en/uk/

Internet Society   www.isoc.org
ITJobsWatch   www.itjobswatch.co.uk
NetJobs.co.uk   www.netjobs.co.uk
NetLingo   www.netlingo.com
Picosearch (search facility)   www.picosearch.com
Secure Computing   www.scmagazine.com/uk/
W3C Worldwide Web Consortium   www.w3.org
WDG – web authoring FAQ   http://htmlhelp.com/faq/html/all.html
Web Developer Jobs (topjobs)   http://web-developer.topjobs.co.uk
Web Developers Virtual Library   www.wdvl.com
Webrec – recruitment agency   www.web-rec.co.uk

DESIGN AND AUDIOVISUAL

See also Chapter 4.
*Note: some of the job agencies listed in other sections may also
hold web designer vacancies.*
Aardman Animations www.aardman.com
AUDIO for the web – podcasting   www.audiofortheweb.com/
why-podcast.html
Blitz Games Studios   www.blitzgamesstudios.com
British Interactive Media Association   www.bima.co.uk
Certified Web Masters Association   www.ciwcertified.com
Datascope – video games and internet jobs   www.datascope.co.uk
Develop   www.developmag.com
Global Games Network   www.edge-online.com
Independent Games Developers Association   www.tiga.org
Keyroutes – web design compare routes   www.keyroutes.org.uk/
careas/itech/opt-wdesign.aspx
New Media Age Jobs   www.nma.co.uk
Podcasting Tools   www.podcasting-tools.com
Skillset – sector skills council for creative media
www.skillset.org/careers/
UK Podcasts   www.ukpodcasts.info
UK Web Design Association   www.ukwda.org
Usability Specialists – see 'Resources'   www.gui-designers.co.uk
VoipReview.org   www.voipreview.org
Web Designer   www.webdesignermag.co.uk
Workingames   www.workingames.co.uk

CONTENT AND INFORMATION

See also Chapter 5.
Associated Northcliffe Digital   www.and.co.uk
Bodington.org – virtual learning open source   www.bodington.org
British Internet Publishers' Alliance   www.bipa.co.uk
Chartered Institute of Library and Information Professionals   www.cilip.org.uk
Chartered Institute of Personnel and Development   www.cipd.co.uk
Digital Content Forum   www.dcf.org.uk
E-Learning   www.guardian.co.uk/education/elearning
Moodle – Course Management System   http://moodle.org
National Union of Journalists   www.nuj.org.uk
Open University – e-learning   www.open.ac.uk/elearning/
People's Network   www.peoplesnetwork.gov.uk
Self-publishing   www.lulu.com
Society for Editors and Proofreaders   www.sfep.org.uk
TFPL   www.tfpl.com
UK Association of Online Publishers   www.ukaop.org.uk
UK Copyright Service   www.copyrightservice.co.uk
UKOLN   www.ukoln.ac.uk

COMMERCIAL AND MARKETING

See also Chapter 6.
Chartered Institute of Marketing   www.cim.co.uk
Direct Marketing Association   www.dma.org.uk
e-consultancy.com   www.e-consultancy.com/jobs/
Institute of Direct Marketing   www.theidm.com
Internet Advertising Bureau   www.iabuk.net
Marketing & Strategy Innovation Blog   http://blog.futurelab.net
Onlinemarketingjobs   www.onlinemarketingjobs.com
Web Marketing   www.marketingguru.co.uk

HOME-WORKING AND SELF-EMPLOYMENT

See also Chapter 7.
Alliance of UK Virtual Assistants   www.allianceofukvirtualassistants.org.uk

CareerAtHome www.careerathome.co.uk
Enterprise Nation http://enterprisenation.com
Flexibility www.flexibility.co.uk
Internet Homeworking Directory www.homeworkinguk.com
National Group of Homeworking www.ngh.org.uk
Ownbase.com www.ownbase.com
Women Investing in Skills for Entrepreneurship www.
  wise4women.co.uk
Workingmums.co.uk www.workingmums.co.uk

TRAINING AND QUALIFICATIONS

See also Chapter 8.
APPRENTICESHIPS
Apprenticeships www.apprenticeships.org.uk
Apprenticeships and Higher Apprenticeships www.e-skills.com/
  apprenticeships
Careersbox www.careersbox.co.uk

THE DIPLOMA
This new qualification for 14–19-year-olds in England is being
  phased in from 2008–2011.
Diplomas AQA – City & Guilds www.diplomainfo.org.uk
Edexcel – the Diploma http://developments.edexcel.org.uk/
  diplomas/
The Diploma – see Diploma details for IT http://yp.direct.gov.uk/
  diplomas/
UCAS – Diplomas www.ucas.com/students/beforeyouapply/
  diplomas/

RESOURCES FOR TEACHERS AND STUDENTS
CC4G – Computer Club for Girls www.cc4g.net
DCSF 14–19 Education and Skills www.dcsf.gov.uk/14-19/
Futurelab www.futurelab.org.uk
ICTeachers www.icteachers.co.uk
National Bureau for Students with Disabilities www.skill.org.uk
RADAR www.radar.org.uk
Specialist Schools and Academies Trust www.specialistschools.
  org.uk

Teacher Resource Exchange   http://tre.ngfl.gov.uk
TechDis   www.techdis.ac.uk

HIGHER EDUCATION
Access to Higher Education   www.accesstohe.ac.uk
Foundation Degree   www.findfoundationdegree.co.uk
Foundation Degree Forward   www.fdf.ac.uk
National IT Learning Centre   www.nitlc.com
Prospectusuk   www.prospectusuk.com
UCAS – Foundation   http://develop.ucas.com/FDCourseSearch/
   About.htm
UCAS – helping students into HE   www.ucas.ac.uk
Internet for ICT – Student Resources   www.vts.intute.ac.uk/he/
   tutorial/ict
Scottish Wider Access Programme   www.scottishwideraccess.org

POSTGRADUATE STUDY AND RESEARCH
Hobsons Postgrad   www.postgrad.hobsons.com
National Postgraduate Committee   www.npc.org.uk
Postgraduate Studentships   www.postgraduatestudentships.co.uk
Prospects – postgrad study   www.prospects.ac.uk
Studylink International   www.studylink.com

DISTANCE AND OPEN LEARNING
Open University   www.open.ac.uk

QUALIFICATIONS AND EXAMINING BOARDS
AQA Guidelines – GCSE and A/AS Level   www.aqa.org.uk/qual
Certificate and Diplomas in Direct and Interactive Marketing   www.
   theidm.com
City & Guilds   www.cityandguilds.com
Department for Employment and Learning Northern Ireland   www.
   delni.gov.uk
Directgov – see Education and Learning Qualifications
   explained   www.direct.gov.uk
Edexcel   www.edexcel.org.uk
Education and Skills – Wales   http://new.wales.gov.uk/topics/
   educationandskills/?lang=en
International Webmasters Association   www.iwanet.org
National Curriculum online   www.nc.uk.net
OCR   www.ocr.org.uk

Qualification and Curriculum Authority   www.qca.org.uk/14-19/
    qualifications
Scottish Qualifications Authority   www.sqa.org.uk
Scottish Vocational Qualifications   www.sqa.org.uk/sqa/2.html
Welsh Joint Education Committee   www.wjec.co.uk

ADDITIONAL PUBLICATIONS

The following list of books and journals may be helpful if you do not
have access to the internet or would prefer to research paper-based
resources. Please note the larger reference books (marked: *ref*) can
be very costly. However, copies should be available in most careers
and Connexion centres and larger public libraries.

A-Z of Careers, The Times
Careers and Jobs in IT, Kogan Page Ltd
Careers 2009 (ref), Trotman
Careers Uncovered: E-Commerce, Trotman
E-Retailing, Charles Dennis, Tino Fenech, Bill Merrilees, Routledge
How to Get Ahead in IT and Administration, Pearson Publishers
    Oxford Ltd
How to Start a Home-based Web Design Business, Jim Smith, Globe
    Pequot Press
Business Jobfile, VT Lifeskills
Real Life Guides: Information and Communication Technology,
    Trotman
Really Useful Compact Guide to Creative Media, Really Useful
    Compact Guide
Really Useful Compact Guide to Information Technology, Really
    Useful Compact Guide
*The Directory and International Direct and E-marketing: A Country
    by Country Sourcebook of Providers, Legislation and Data*,
    Roderick Millar, Kogan Page Ltd
*The eBay Business Handbook: How Anyone Can Build a Business
    and Make Money on eBay.co.uk*, Robert Pugh, Harriman House Ltd
*The New Rules of Marketing and PR: How to Use News Releases,
    Blogs, Podcasting, Viral Marketing and Online Media to Reach
    Buyers*, David Meerman Scott, John Wiley and Sons Inc
Directly Web Design: The Complete Reference, Thomas Powell,
    Osbourne/McGraw-Hill
Working in Creative Media, VT Lifeskills